The Table Maker

The Table Maker

A Carpenter's Guide to Life

JOEL BIRD

Published by 535
An imprint of Blink Publishing

2.25, The Plaza,
535 Kings Road,
Chelsea Harbour,
London, SW10 0SZ

www.blinkpublishing.co.uk

facebook.com/blinkpublishing
twitter.com/blinkpublishing

Hardback – 978-1-788-700-03-0
Ebook – 978-1-788-700-04-7

A CIP catalogue of this book is available from the British Library.

Designed by Steve Leard
Printed and bound by Druk-Intro

1 3 5 7 9 10 8 6 4 2

Blink Publishing is an imprint of Bonnier Books UK
www.bonnierbooks.co.uk

'The highest reward for a person's toil is not what they get for it, but what they become by it'.

JOHN RUSKIN

Contents

Introduction
Not All Tables are Made Equal

Introduction

'Remain sitting at your table and listen.
Do not even listen, simply wait, be quiet,
still and solitary. The world will freely offer
itself to you to be unmasked, it has no
choice, it will roll in ecstasy at your feet.'

FRANZ KAFKA

The act of working with your hands to bring an object into existence is a special experience. The skills and techniques, the tools and materials involved are all interesting, but they do not tell the whole story. Making something from start to finish offers us the increasingly rare opportunity to connect, not just with the world around us, but with the traditions and cultures of our past.

When I decided to write this book, I wanted to pass on my knowledge of working with wood, but I also wanted to include the philosophy of carpentry and introduce some of the more spiritual aspects associated with crafting traditions. I decided the best way to achieve this was to use the making of an object as a means to understand more about life. I wanted the object to be in some way useful and what better choice than, for me the most useful object of all, the humble table.

The table is many things: a place to eat, a surface to write or draw, a setting in which to negotiate or philosophise. It is a social hub where people get to know each other or a quiet refuge where we can get to know ourselves. My fondest childhood memories, and indeed many important moments throughout my life, are closely associated with this raised wooden surface. For me, the table not only evokes being together for family meals, but long hours of happy solitude, drawing and thinking and imagining. To this day I feel at home at a table, I relate it to peaceful contemplation or the excitement of a new project.

However, not all tables are made equal. Most of us in our early explorations of home furnishings have owned the mass-produced, flat-pack, chipboard table garnished with wood veneer, which pretends to be sound but is weak limbed and has difficulty withstanding the weight of a large meal. Eventually we come to realise that the things we like and choose to have around us say something about who we are.

There are some tables that have made an impression on me, not always for good reasons. My auntie had a flamboyant, mint green, oval table with elaborately curved ornamental legs that demanded to be the focal point of any room, but it was all brace plates, no tenons and, despite the high price tag, it was reluctantly discarded because no one actually wanted to spend time with it.

The table that fixed my opinions was the one that adorned the living room of my friend's parents. It was a deep red-brown, probably mahogany, with a shiny French-polished exterior. It had the uncomfortable presence of something fragile but not beautiful. One day its perfectly veneered surface was ever so slightly scratched much to the fury of his parents, and I remember thinking this is not a table, it's just pretending to be one, it's an ornament. When an object ceases to function in the way it was designed, it must be relegated to the realms of the superficial or indeed the useless.

The tables I like are quiet. They sit patiently waiting for the day's purpose to reveal itself. They offer themselves to a room, not attempting to grab attention or dominate, inconspicuous in their simplicity, saving their qualities for those who are interested. The table that I grew up with was one such example. A simple 5ft x 3ft pine table, four legs joined with mortise and tenon joints, and a wide apron to support decent dimensions. It was given to us by my uncle in the 1960s when he was clearing out the old main post office in Whitechapel, Liverpool. Who knows how long it stood there, probably since the 1920s or 1930s, which would make it close to a hundred years old. It still sits as composed as ever in my parents' dining room. It has participated in the raising of two generations, who ate and grew and learned at its surface and there is no reason why it won't participate in two more. I wonder whether an object such as this can be described as having a soul? It depends how you see the world, but it certainly claimed the respect and perhaps even love of our family.

Thinking back, I suspect the relationship I had with this table helped to nourish my love for woodwork and wooden objects, so much so that when I started a family of my own I felt an urge to make a table for us. I was no stranger to carpentry, my day job was and still is to make bespoke wooden structures for people to live and work in. These buildings are always very different and are individually designed to fit a purpose or a particular personality, but a table is different – its power lies in its basic yet versatile form. Although a table looks simple, there are qualities that often go unseen. Knowledge of the component parts and how they are made enhances a table's beauty, but true appreciation comes from taking part in the making process itself.

Something happens when you make an object that is difficult to fully understand until you have experienced it. The act of working with your hands to accomplish a series of tasks, the ability to simplify your thoughts and the focus required to do a job well with skill and accuracy brings out the best in you. In these solitary moments of work, it feels as though time has stopped, as if nature is showing you that there is peace in the world if you will just allow yourself to see it. Throughout the process you see the fruits of your labour and to step back and cast your eye over something that you have brought into the world brings feelings of not just accomplishment, but a sense of purpose and well-being.

The aim of this book is to pass on the skills of table making while also expressing the personal journey that accompanies the learning of these skills. It is part textbook, part meditation – it has within its pages the information needed to make a quality table of your own, and I hope that at the end of reading it you will appreciate how adopting some of the philosophies of the maker can change the way you view the world.

A note on measurements

At this point, I would like to briefly explain something about measurements. There will be times in this book when I am using imperial measurements, at others metric and sometimes I will use both. This inconsistency is not through any lackadaisical shortcomings; the use of a particular measurement will be related to the circumstances involved. I have tried to make the measurements compatible and consistent with each other but the fact is, people use different systems depending on their own area of expertise as well as which part of the world they are living and working. For example, some of the traditional sizes of wood and the machinery that is used to cut the wood are designed with imperial measurements in mind. The workers who use these machines will understand imperial measurement and there would be little point in me converting these sizes to metric. On other occasions, some wood sizes will be supplied in metric and for me personally when I am dealing with smaller sizes, I find the metric system less confusing. In terms of my table, the overall dimensions are not an exact science and since the table design I have chosen is one that goes back hundreds of years, the imperial system often feels appropriate.

Part 1
Table
Beginnings

The Ash tree and the Alaskan mill

I had found a tree. For months I had been asking the people I know who work with wood in its various forms if they could recommend a good source of timber from which to make my table. I had wanted to find some seasoned, preferably indigenous, hardwood to work on, but a call from my cousin in Matlock, Derbyshire changed this, as he explained that he had met a couple of local guys who had cut down a large Ash tree that had become dangerous. My response was immediate. 'Let's go for it!' The idea of going right back to the source of the wood was more interesting and I felt that seeing the actual tree that my table would come from would only increase my connection to the whole experience.

I booked my train to take the East Coast Line from London to Darley Dale in Derbyshire on the edge of the Peak District. Generally speaking I don't consider myself to be the most dramatic of characters, but the idea of getting hold of a large chunk of tree felt quite thrilling, and the night before I left, I was so excited that I barely slept. Once in Derbyshire, my cousin and I drove through winding country roads to see Shaun and Richard from Natural Earth Woodcraft where the tree was being stored.

It is a beautiful morning in late September, the leaves are just starting to redden and gently scatter the fields as autumn begins to assert itself on the rural landscape. We are deep into Derbyshire's agricultural land, where the vistas are filled with the hills and valleys of the Peak District National Park. Much of the park is farmland, but in parts it is wild and untamed, yet the landscape feels at once familiar and imbued with the power to reorder thoughts and impose peace. It is good to be out of the city and as we drive I am reminded of how important it will become to preserve and manage these landscapes, so that future generations can experience the same feelings as we do.

When it comes to a natural sense of direction, my cousin Robbie has a similar deficiency to me. He explains to me that the last time he visited Shaun and Richard he navigated his way by a cloud of smoke visible from miles away, created by the charcoaling of the offcuts and scraps of wood from the pair's work. Eventually we enter a field through the back of a derelict farmhouse and walk a passage through logs and machinery towards a roundhouse constructed from wood.

We are greeted with a cup of tea made from a Ghillie kettle, a useful little device which dates back to the early 1900s when it was used for boiling water with scraps of wood, making it the perfect companion for a place such as this. The roundhouse (it's actually octagonal) is a cacophony of woodworking tools, chainsaw blades, sawhorses, wood blocks and power tools. Light enters through an old window, but there are also electric-powered lanterns which make the place feel part grotto. A wood burner stands next to an old tree stump coffee table with an axe embedded in its surface ready to make kindling. We stand inside the walls of the building on a thick carpet of sawdust. Above us is a circular roof made from uncut tree timbers that congregate at the centre into an old car wheel, through which the wood burner flue exited. It's a magical place. If you could dream up the workshop of a woodcrafter, this would basically be it. I briefly explain my table-making project and am met with the typical enthusiasm I often get from people who work with their hands, then it was off to see the tree.

We walk to the top of the hill and although the tree was cut into four or five pieces, I could see immediately how large it had once been. One of these pieces sat at the very top of the hill next to a drystone wall which marked the boundary of the next field. This was my piece of tree, an Ash. It was already cut in half down its length, exposing the full surface, and had sat here for almost a year. Although it had been exposed to the rain, it had also been exposed to the wind and the sun and through the summer months this would have hopefully aided the drying process. It is strange how even the benign objects of the natural world can make us feel sometimes. As I stood next to my tree, the sheer mass of this once-living organism impacted me viscerally like a great rock or an animal carcass.

The tree had originally sat next to the boundary of a farm, which might account for why it had been left alone to grow and had survived for so long. Trees at the edge of a boundary do not need to be cleared for agricultural

purposes, as often the ambiguity of ownership preserves them, and the longer a tree lives the more potential it has to nourish affection. This tree's demise was due to rot at its centre making it unstable, and since it stood next to a clutch of three or four houses, the danger of the tree falling of its own accord and destroying everything in its fall path posed too great a risk. It also sat in a place called 'Windy Fields', which didn't bode well for a rotting tree's long-term survival chances.

When we look into the end of the bottom piece of the tree, we can see that a good third has rotted, and peering inside the hole at the base of the tree revealed that it was filled with honeycomb. Trees are the driving force of biodiversity in forest ecosystems. They provide a huge source of potential energy, and if a tree is left to rot naturally, the transference of this energy has an effect on everything from soil nutrients to wildlife populations, but it is interesting to see evidence of a tree providing a physical habitat for wildlife, in this case wild bees. It also occurred to me that the bee colony could have made their home here many years ago and the tree grew around them, meaning that the base was always hollow and one day it just became too weak to support the tree's mass.

We count the rings of the next slab of tree, reaching 150 before the centre of the tree splits into two rings. This means that, all in, the tree was at least 150 years old. Although not the most ancient of trees, it's age was significant enough, especially for an Ash tree. The average lifespan of a British Ash is 100–150 years. It rarely exceeds 250 years, but some can live as long as 400 years and if coppiced many hundreds of years more. When this tree was beginning to grow it would have been around the 1860s. To give this a little historical reference, this was the time of Abraham Lincoln, the American Civil War, the writings of Charles Dickens, the emergence of the Impressionist painters, the music of Richard Wagner and the politics of Karl Marx. It was also before the automobile, the incandescent light bulb and the two-stroke chainsaw.

It is time to cut. Shaun and Richard fix their Stihl® chainsaw onto what is commonly referred to as an Alaskan mill. This consists of a pair of rails which are attached to the bar of a chainsaw. The rails then ride on the top of the tree surface allowing the chainsaw to cut at a consistent depth. It is a wide piece of tree – the width of the plank which can be cut is determined by the length of the bar which is anything up to 34in. In fact, our tree exceeds this size, so first Richard cuts a bulbous section from the side of the trunk to make using the mill possible. This is a two-man procedure with one person on either side of the tree in order to keep the chainsaw blade perpendicular to the direction it is cutting in.

The cutting starts and immediately sawdust streams into the autumn air like a tiny snowstorm. The kerf or width of the saw cut is relatively large on a chainsaw, which creates a lot of dust. This is no problem when cutting large pieces like the ones I require but it would mean significant waste if cutting lots of thin boards. When using an Alaskan mill a ripping chain is used, rather than the usual chain designed for cross-cuts. The cutters on the ripping chain are set between 0 and 5 degrees as opposed to a standard cross-cut chain where the teeth are at 35 degrees. In addition to this, every third or fourth cutter is a third of the width which means less friction, so the cutting speed is increased.

They are roughly a fifth of the way through cutting my section of the tree when progress slows. After checking the width of the tree again to ensure it was still not too wide for the mill, it is decided that the blade is not quite up to it, so it is back to the roundhouse for a sharpen. The sawdust snowstorm could have been a sign. If fine dust is coming from your chainsaw it can mean the chain needs sharpening, whereas chips indicate the cutters are sharp. For me, it is useful to see all the processes involved in cutting the tree, so going back to sharpen the blade made the experience all the more interesting. You can sharpen a chain using a mixture of round and flat files and a depth gauge, but it is quicker to use a multi-tool with a blade-sharpening attachment, and Shaun has such a device ready. After removing the chain, there followed a period of short bursts of sparks as the grinder removed glowing particles of steel dust and reshaped the teeth, bringing the chain back to life. We are quickly back in business.

I have worked in environments such as these before and in the successful ones there is often very little fuss. Although workshops may function in very different ways, there is an attitude which is always the same – an unspoken rule. I would describe it as respect, not just for the situation, but for time. It is as though the very concept of a 'problem' is not tolerated – it is not allowed to exist. There is work to be done, to sharpen the blade is the most efficient means to complete the task of cutting the tree – it is the simple fact of the matter, like drinking water when you are thirsty or working in the light-filled hours.

Back at the Ash tree the Alaskan mill returns to work. The blade is cutting more easily now and progress is swift. As the mill cuts, wedges are placed between the top slab and the rest of the tree, to take pressure off the chainsaw blade. Once through the trunk, it is time to move it. The slab is just over 4in thick and with this substantial weight it takes all four of us to lift it. Shaun and Richard talk about the revealing of the grain and how we will be the first people ever to see it. We slide the slab next to the trunk to marvel at the unique pattern that nature had designed over many years of slow growth.

We stand the slab upright for a photograph; at 7ft high and 3ft wide it is quite a piece of wood and it already looks like a table top. It had been suggested to me, even before I had found a tree, that it would be great to make a one-piece table top because of how beautiful it would look and this slab of wood would certainly be enough to make one. However, I had always intended to make a table of conventional design and I wanted to stick to my guns. Besides, in reality, a table top made from separate planks would be more stable and it would be less likely to move and warp, especially when compared to a thick piece of wood that still needs drying.

This first 4in slab was for the legs; we now need to cut two more slabs for the top boards, the aprons, rails and a stretcher, this time at a width of 2in. With the newly sharpened chain, the next two slabs seem to get cut in no

time. The tree is now half the size. Richard works out the cost by calculating the amount of wood. In total there is 9.67ft3. The trunk now lies there. We have taken the prime cuts and the great carcass is diminished, but just like a carcass, every last scrap of wood on this tree would be used. Richard and Shaun would fashion a wood block, or spare handles, or even just firewood to keep them warm in the workshop through the winter months. The last morsels would be used to make biochar – a carbon-rich soil amendment, which has a long list of qualities including increased fertility in soils, improved water quality, enhanced disease resistance and increased agricultural productivity. Making biochar is also a practice that captures and stores carbon dioxide by carbon sequestration (one way to defer global warming), which ties in to the whole eco credentials of this place. And besides, nature doesn't waste – in environments such as these the tree will still decompose and eventually enter the structure of the soil.

It takes all four of us to load the slabs into my cousin's van and it is off to the roundhouse workshop for a last cup of tea before we leave. I now have three magnificent pieces of wood, and the sense of purpose that accompanies beginnings – an excitement that this is now happening, and for me, there is nothing quite like the feeling of starting a new project.

Plato's table

'If particulars are to have meaning, there
must be universals.'

PLATO

Over the years I have thought a great deal about the humble table, what
makes the perfect design and what would be the best way to build it. I have
adapted and simplified and re-adapted designs to try to understand the table.
I have considered the perfect practical and aesthetic dimension – a length to
neatly fit two chairs either side, a width that will allow enough room to eat
in comfort, a short enough distance to reach the centre of the table top from
any position, but large enough to be supremely useful. I have thought about
the best structure – a design that is not too expensive and is simple to make,
but is strong and long lasting. I have researched the best woods to use: Pine
for its accessibility and value, Beech for its hardness and durability or Oak
for its moisture stability and high tensile strength. I have even gone as far as
to try to create a formula for the most aesthetically pleasing leg taper ratio.

It becomes clear when studying the history of table design that
carpenters through time have also carefully considered these aspects and
many designs that appear at first glance to be basic, are in fact the final
destination of a long series of subtle adaptations. Conceptually I often
think of the table as a raised floor. It is of course possible to make a table by
placing a rock on a tree stump, but it is the destiny of all things to become
more stable. The base structures, the joints, the dimensions, the wood-
preserving techniques all develop in an attempt to strengthen or extend life.
Just as evolution in nature preserves improvements and discards flaws, so too
does design. The process of change goes on and on, sometimes backwards,
sometimes forwards, over and over until at some point the evolution stops.

The point at which things remain the same is just as interesting as the process of change. Sometimes we focus on the aspects of life that are continually in flux, and we forget the parts of life that have become efficient and stable, approaching a state of perfection. I sometimes think objects or entities that reach this point are the inevitable consequences of time. It is almost as if a kind of truth enters the fabric of their being and, for me, the table is the perfect example of this.

It makes me think of Plato's concepts of ideal forms. Plato raised the question of how we would recognise the correct or perfect form of anything, a form that would be true for all people for all time. He stated that we can imagine the perfect triangle or straight line or circle but that these perfect forms cannot exist in a changing material world. His conclusion was that there must be a world of perfect ideas or forms that is eternal and immutable that we can only perceive through our reason. Sometimes I think of the table as an intermediate between the two worlds. A form that has evolved to a perfect state and now has something of the eternal within it and at the same time exists in the material world and is subject to the same laws of decay and change.

To see the beauty of a simple but perfectly formed object sometimes takes a little learning – the more we understand about an object, the more we appreciate it. In the case of a table, understanding the origins of a particular design and the purposes for which the design developed helps to grow this appreciation.

The table I am interested in making for this project is really just a variation on the trestle table, a design which goes right back to the medieval times and quite possibly many hundreds of years before this. These early tables were lightweight and sturdy, they provided the greatest amount of stability with the least amount of materials. In the Middle Ages there was often no room dedicated to dining so these tables were designed to be collapsible. By simply removing the pegs in the stretches, the tables could be quickly and easily dismantled to make space. These trestle tables were often quite narrow because diners did not usually sit across from each other. Sitting on one side allowed easy access to servers and in the event of an attack in these turbulent times it also meant the table could be flipped on its side and used as protection. As the world expanded, the trestle table remained popular because it was able to be packed down and transported which avoided trying to buy or to make new tables.

In the later Middle Ages, a more permanent table design developed for banquet rooms or feasting in the great halls of noble residences. This

table became known as the refectory table, beginning in monasteries as a place at which large congregations of monks could take their meals. It was structurally more superior, often very long and, with two legs per trestle instead of one, the table had more support which allowed for an increase in the table width – this design has changed very little to the present day (*below*: the elongated refectory table in noble residences).

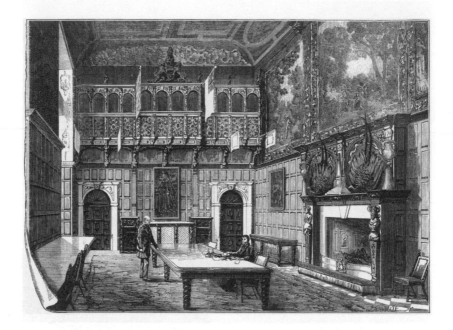

The subsequent years of technical sophistication meant tables began to reflect the design tendencies of their period. The decoration and embellishment of the late seventeenth and eighteenth centuries is not particularly relevant to this project, and although the craftsmanship of this period is obviously something that can be admired, I must admit that this design opulence, which was a way in which to display the wealth of the table owners, is not something I am especially interested in.

Many of the simple table designs of earlier periods remained out of favour for hundreds of years. These utilitarian works of art sat quietly, waiting gracefully in the shadows for their elegance to be rediscovered, which it finally was with the emergence of the Arts and Crafts movements of Europe and America. There would again be fluctuations of fashion and desires to appeal to the wealthy through the curves and details of the Art Nouveau and Art Deco periods, but the subtle beauty of a perfectly designed table can never be destroyed by fashion and today it can be said that the simple and functional aesthetic has earned a permanent place in our design vocabulary.

And so this philosophy forms the basis of the design I will be concentrating on. An emphasis on material, structure and function – an efficient piece of furniture that expresses the aesthetic of beautiful design without making it more important than the specific use of the furniture. My table will consist of a top made from separate boards to give my table surface stability. It will comprise four square legs, with simple but well-proportioned connecting aprons, and supporting the legs at the base will be rails on the short width. Between these rails a long stretcher will give the table maximum strength. It all will be fitted together with well-made and sturdy mortise and tenon joints. Although I expect to use power tools along the way, it is perfectly possible to make this table with hand tools just as it was crafted many hundreds of years ago.

This table design is strong, it is fit for purpose, it is constructed to endure, it has earned its place in this world and our respect for it should begin at the point of its existence. It is a design which reflects the ideal, it expresses the quiet integrity and dignity we should seek within ourselves and in doing so it allows these elusive qualities to become more tangible.

Trestle Table for Six

Qty	Part	Size	Notes
6	TOP BOARDS	2"×6"×70"	
4	LEGS	4"×4"×30"	
2	LONG APRONS	2"×3"×68"	64" BETWEEN TENON SHOULDERS
2	SHORT APRONS	2"×3"×34"	30" BETWEEN TENON SHOULDERS
2	BOTTOM RAILS	2"×3"×34"	" " " "
1	STRETCHER	2"×3"×68"	64" BETWEEN TENON SHOULDERS
2	SPARES	2"×3"×68"	" " " "

The carpenter's sketchbook

'Drawing is putting a line around an idea.'

HENRI MATISSE

The carpenter's sketchbook is a wonderful thing, housing the scrawls of a mind at work, busy considering the practical and aesthetic implications of ideas as a person journeys closer to their destination. Its pages offer a place to explore, to discard wrong turns, to distil thoughts and, eventually, a place in which to make ideas real and transform them into concrete plans with numbers and sizes and fixings and joints. You should embrace the concept of the carpenter's sketchbook; it has been around since the beginning of carpentry for a reason.

With my table design in place, it is time to sharpen my pencil and think about proportions. Proportions, as I will explain, involve a deceptively complex set of circumstances, but as with anything in life, negotiating a path through many variables involves learning to simplify and focusing on what matters.

The size of your table is dependent on the size of the room your table will be in, the number of people that are likely to use the table at one time and the functions you expect the table to fulfil. In the case of my table, I have an idea of where the table will go, but I want it to have the potential to be used in other smaller rooms. I want the table to be multifunctional but since dining generally takes up the most room of the intended functions then this takes priority in deciding the size. I have a family of four, but as others often visit, I want the smallest possible table that is going to comfortably sit four people for dinner and is capable, on occasion, of sitting six people.

I will explain the implications this has on my design and my logic in approaching the solution. The room I have in mind for my table is roughly

11ft (3.35m) x 14ft (4.27m), but I intend to have furniture along one wall which will leave a floor space of 9ft (2.75m) x 14ft (4.27m). Ideally there should be 3ft (92cm) around the table so there is space for others to pass by and also enough room to easily pull the chair away from the table and stand up. This leaves a space of 3ft (92cm) x 8ft (244cm), so this is the area I have to work with or, in other words, this is roughly the maximum size my table should be. I want my table to be efficient on materials and labour time and, from my own perspective, the idea of making the smallest possible table without losing any of its objectives also signifies a successful design. When deciding on size it is worth remembering what we are actually measuring. It is not an arbitrary judgement of size based only on the size of the room; what we are really measuring is people and the space people need to function in comfort.

Most tables are about 30in (76cm) from floor to surface; this has changed very little over the years, only growing slightly to accommodate the increase in size of people. From floor to apron there should be a minimum of 26in (70cm) to accommodate legs and knees. The minimum place setting is around 22in (56cm) in width and 13in (33cm) in depth, but I also want it to be possible to seat a person on the short lengths of the table, so in total the sensible minimum length of my table should be 22in + 22in + 13in + 13in = 70in (178cm). This also means when extra guests are not eating, there will be a more comfortable space for four diners. Using a similar logic for the width, I will need a minimum of 13in (33cm) + 13in (33cm) for the place setting of two people opposite each other and I want to leave another 10in (26cm) for the centre of the table in which food or drinks can be placed or room for things like gravy boats and candlesticks. This leads me to a minimum width of around 36in (91cm) which is quite a standard size for a table. At this width it means the centre stretcher will not be in the way of people's feet when seated. It also allows a standard chair to be pushed completely underneath the table so that it takes up the minimum amount of space when not in use.

As you can see, it is not necessarily just as simple as measuring your room. I have explained my logic behind the proportions for my table given its purpose in life. Your table may well be different, but you should think about these types of things prior to cutting to get the best results. The carpenter's sketchbook is the best place to start your thinking. It is important to see all the workings out written down for reference and to examine and re-examine your solutions, as this process will help you to make better decisions. When starting out on your design, your drawings should be free flowing, they should be approximations and they should express your ideas in a rough form.

Dining Table for Six

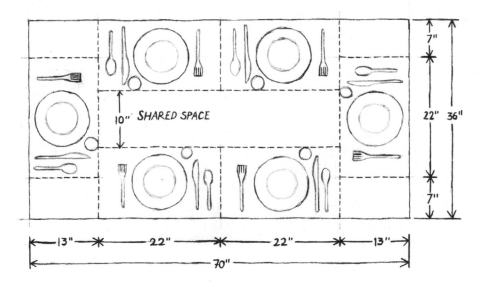

SHARED SPACE

10"

7"

22" 36"

7"

13"   22"   22"   13"

70"

As time goes on and your ideas become more settled, you can condense your drawings into something that is easily understood. Make your final drawings clutter free, with only the essential measurements. For example, there is little point in writing down the size of both lengths of the table top or all four legs since you know they are parallel and of the same size.

When I am happy with my design and the sizes, I like to draw my table from above, from the side and from the front. On the above view I split the table into boards so I can work out how many I will need and at what size. The side and front views remind me of each of the component parts and the sizes. Next I draw each of these component parts separately so that I can be sure I haven't missed anything and from these I make what is known as a cut list.

Your cut list should consist of four columns: PART, SIZE, QUANTITY, NOTES. Always give your work headings, so you can quickly find and understand what you are referencing when looking over your notes. Name your parts properly so there is no confusion; when you are writing down sizes, the width is the direction across the wood grain, the length is the direction of the grain and be consistent with either inches or centimetres to avoid confusion. In the notes section you can write down information such as whether you have included spares, the size of the tenons, whether the wood will be exposed or part of a joint, etc. Ultimately, write down whatever you think is going to make your life easier when referencing your cut list.

The sizes in your cut list are your finished sizes, and these are what you will consider when buying prepared wood that has already been planed. If, like me, you are starting from wood in its raw state, then before having it cut to size you will need to add a bit extra to all the dimensions. It is better to be oversized and have to work a little to cut it down, than be undersized and left to make do. There are many adages in carpentry such as 'measure twice, cut once' and 'as long as you can for as long as you can' – keep these in mind when you are setting off to the workshop to have your cuts made.

The first cuts

'The beginning is the most important part
of the work.'

PLATO

We are back at my cousin's workshop, known as Darley Barn. It sits between his house and his farmland on the borders of the Peak District. This is where we will be building our table, partly because of the space in the workshop and its picturesque surroundings, but also because the area has many tradesmen and industries connected with woodwork and forestry. I helped Robbie build this workshop; it was built on the stone walls of an old swimming pool (which always seemed an unusual setting for such a construction). It is a substantial size at around 60m², but with its blackened timber cladding and its traditional Norwegian sod roof, it is quiet and unassuming to the passing eye. It sits in harmony with the rugged surroundings, so much so that you barely notice it until you are right up close. It is quite high in the hills of Derbyshire where the weather feels exaggerated. My memories of working here are infused with feelings about conditions that were at times relentlessly cold, in which fine rain seized the finger joints and made me want to retreat indoors, and, at others, so enticing that I couldn't wait to get started, to be outdoors in the crisp, early sunlight. I am expecting it will be a similar experience for the table-making project.

The van sits outside still weighed down with tree. Robbie has a decent table saw that he feels has the power to get through the smaller slabs so we lift these into the workshop. The larger one is going to need a bigger, more powerful machine, so there is little point trying to manhandle it with just the two of us. Armed with my cut list, we set about drawing each of the component parts onto the slabs. These pencil marks are only rough guides

to ensure we have enough wood available. On the two smaller slabs we mark out the boards. Since the slabs were around 60cm wide and 170cm in length, we manage to get six boards at 17cm x 170cm, which would easily give us enough for the 90cm width table I require. For the large slab we crawl into the van and mark out the four legs. Since the legs are to be 76cm in height we are able to get all four legs in two runs, while the rest would be the aprons, the rails and the central stretcher, which we duly mark up.

Robbie's friend Pete runs a large workshop called Ashton and Coleman that makes beautifully crafted handmade furniture. He had met him through his daughter's school and had spoken to him that morning on the school run. That is how these places are to me – although there are fewer people than in cities, it feels as though there is more connection. The residents know what each other does for a living and they find their own particular niche to survive. People will also swap skills or help out to get things done, so it feels much more like I imagine communities were in times gone by.

We drive a couple of miles to Two Dales in Matlock, where Pete's workshop is. On arrival the slab is lifted with the help of Pete onto a trolley and wheeled through the shop section of the building into a large workshop at the back. This place immediately feels more organised and industrial than the roundhouse; it is clean and tidy, but it still has charm, with beautiful old machinery, half-crafted furniture and a mix of powered and hand tools organised around the wall space.

We explain the project to Pete and the cuts we want from the slab. He seems to approve of the design of the table. It is not a dissimilar design to the pieces of furniture around us, in that it concentrated on a simple and well-proportioned form. Pete voices some concerns over the fact that it is a large piece of wood and he explains that Ash doesn't actually tend to twist much, but that a large piece like this would potentially have some tension in it, which might lead it to warp or split. However, Pete doesn't seem to be too worried. 'At the end of the day it's only Ash, so if you do need another piece you can go and get one and it will still fit with it. You know, if you've got some strange exotic timber you'd be a bit more worried. And to be honest you would often use what you had in the old days, that's why in older furniture you get different types of wood put together – you would use what was available and make it work. It wasn't so designed. You know, it would be like, there's a tree down, so let's make something out of it, as opposed to let's cut a tree down.'

Pete measures the slab and on closer inspection, the slab thickness turns out to be 110mm, so the finished table leg should be 90mm and we leave

extra so it can be planed down to size. The problem with this is that the table saw they have in the workshop, although powerful enough to get through the slab, is only able to cut through a thickness just shy of 4in(10cm), which would mean two passes through the machine. They decide to try and use the bandsaw instead, but there is some uncertainty as to whether it will have the power to cut through such a large piece of wood. Pete and the other workers begin by changing the blade, which is a long, serrated strip of flexible, steel ribbon. The machine stands 8ft tall or more, reminding me of an oversized spool on a sewing machine, but with all of its muscular power, it is not cumbersome and is still beautiful to watch – a grace which comes from its efficiency as a machine. Next, they spray down the table surface of the bandsaw with a thin coat of WD40 to reduce the friction when pushing the wood through the machine.

The bandsaw is powered up and whirrs into action. As the speed of the blade increases, so too does the pitch, and I could only just about hear Pete over the noise. 'These old machines are great, no bells or whistles. They're not actually that expensive compared to newer ones, but it's just keeping them running. This one is around 70 years old and still going the way it was back when it was made.'

It takes four of us to the lift the slab onto the surface. It is green wood (undried) and it still has the weight of the water inside it. The first cut follows a pencil mark straight down the centre of the slab. Pete explains that this should take some of the tension out of the wood and ultimately reduce waste on the surfacer. Cutting through the centre of the slab would give us two pieces that were easier to manoeuvre. Pete guides the slab along the pencil line and it takes two more men to help pull the weight. Next Pete runs it down the surfacer, another beautiful old machine – a burly mix of cast iron and polished steel. This would get a straight edge to work from, so we could then run the wood down the fence (the straight edge that is placed parallel to the direction of the blade) on the bandsaw. With our new lighter wood and with the help of the fence, the rest of the passes are straightforward. Perhaps the bandsaw wasn't the ideal choice, but it worked perfectly, and Pete's team seemed to think the cuts wouldn't have been possible if it wasn't green wood, so in this case it helped that it wasn't dry. Our wood is now cut to size; in one respect it is sad to see the great slab chopped into morsels, but great to know we had completed another stage of the process.

We had spent a fair amount of time in the workshop and had help from a good number of people, though when I offered payment Pete said he was just happy to be of assistance. For me it was great just being around all of these magnificent old machines still working the way they would have all those years ago, but the experience was further enhanced by the generosity of time and spirit by all the workers here. We load up the wood into the van and head off to buy a crate of ale for the workshop lads and ladies. Back at Robbie's, with the help of another new blade, we use his table saw to cut the boards from the 2in slabs and by the end of the working day, we have all the wood we need ready for the next stage.

The story
of a tree

'I am myself and my circumstances.'

JOSÉ ORTEGA Y GASSET

To be able to look at a piece of wood and understand what it is telling you is a skill and a gift. The tightness in the grain, the way the lines of growth are shaped, the colours between these layers of growth, the knots, the twists, even the disease within the wood – all these elements make up the story of the tree. Interpreting them reveals something of the tree's life and from this you can deduce the strengths and weaknesses in the wood and you can work out how the wood wants to be treated. For example, when we marked out the legs on my slab of wood, it was important to look for long, consistent grain lines in the same direction as the legs – these lines tell us the way the wood has grown, and the way the wood has grown during the tree's life is the way the wood will naturally exist thereafter.

When we talk about the tension in the wood, as we did in the last chapter, we are really describing how the tree has adjusted to forces in its life, the most influential of which is gravity. The tree will produce different types of wood depending on the angles and directions it has grown in. For example, wood under tension will often have more cellulose in it, whereas wood under compression will have more lignin. This wood is often known as reaction wood. It helps to maintain the various angles and makes the tree stronger and more able to cope with its environment, but when it is no longer a tree, this reaction wood can sometimes twist or warp. I think of it rather like potential energy which accumulates in the tree during its life and when the tree is cut, the energy wants to release and become stable.

When we reshape this wood, as we will eventually do with my wood, by using a surfacer and a thicknesser to get it straight, we are adapting and changing the tree, but it is important to remain aware of the way the wood wants to be. We choose a suitable piece of wood by understanding that the things that have happened in the wood's past will define the potential the wood has for change in the future. If a piece of wood is forced to change too much, it will inevitably want to return to its natural state. You learn to be receptive to materials in carpentry because if you are not, a piece can be ruined, and the more you are receptive to the world around you, the more this perspective penetrates other areas of your life. There are times when I have used my knowledge of wood to help solve more nebulous problems I have faced. For example in times of grief I have become a harder person in order to still function, but being aware of this change can help to avoid it being a permanent disposition.

The Spanish philosopher José Ortega y Gasset, born 1883, in his Meditations on Quixote wrote: 'I am myself and my circumstances.' He believed that our reason should be used to understand the circumstances we find ourselves in, so we can change our lives for the better. Many people, he says, live without reflecting on their circumstances, but striving to understand our circumstances exposes the assumptions which lie behind our beliefs. He says that if we want to think about how we should be in this world, we should understand that we are always immersed in circumstances that are shaped by our past and our habits. This habitual thinking runs deep and there is a limit to the extent to which we can change because of these circumstances. Even if we free ourselves to imaging new possibilities, the future will always collide with the reality of the way we are now.

I sometimes think about how much I adjust my life in this world to adapt to situations or to other people. It is always good to challenge ourselves and to question the various beliefs we have but, as time goes on, we also need to try to put ourselves in the right positions in the first place to make life run smoother.

I am reminded of the Japanese wooden building traditions of using timber for different purposes depending on where and how it has grown to take advantage of its inherent qualities. For example, trees that have grown on the top of a mountain are more likely to be straight and strong and these would be ideal for structural timber. The trees that have grown on the lower part of the mountain slope are often straight but thin, so although they are not suitable for columns or beams, they are still useful for

exposed elements because they often have fewer knots. The trees that have grown in windy areas or on steep slopes can sometimes be curved and bent and a skilful carpenter uses these to weave together archways, decorative structural columns or beams. Similarly, according to this ancient tradition, trees grown on the north-facing slopes of the mountain were placed on the north side of a building; the same principle would be used for timber with a southern exposure.

How a tree has grown also affects the way the forces will naturally flow through the wood. The Japanese wood builders would take this into account, so that when the wood was used as columns it would be positioned root side down and canopy up, just as it had grown in the forest. If two timbers were needed to make a vertical column, then the canopy end of the timber would be joined to the root end which allowed the natural stresses to continue in a single direction.

Potentially every piece of a tree could be used, from the thick columns of a tall mountain tree for framework, right down to weak and twisted timber for interesting decorative patterns. Even the bark of certain trees was used in construction for elements such as roofing or for making the washi paper internal walls – it was all about understanding the various properties of the wood and utilising them in the way that naturally served their innate properties best.

I like to think that we can apply this same philosophy to modern-day carpentry and beyond into how we engage with the people in our lives. We all have innate qualities and experiences that have shaped our growth. Understanding these allows us to get the best out of everyone and every situation – both inside and outside the workshop.

Sourcing
your timber

I had wanted to start the table from as early in the process as possible because I felt it would give me a deeper understanding of wood as a living organism and not just a material. However, starting from the tree stage does make the project more complicated because of the seasoning process which needs to take place over time to make the wood stable enough to work with. If you don't have the luxury of time, then buying pre-seasoned wood from a supplier is going to be more straightforward. Still, there are some things to be aware of when buying wood.

Where you choose to buy your timber depends on the type of wood you intend to use. If you are buying softwood for your table which is primarily going to be pine then it should be possible to buy from any local builders merchant. They may also be able to order other types of wood in for you, but since they are acting as a middle man, you may pay a premium for this type of arrangement.

Do not discount softwoods which can be cost effective and manageable but if it is quality you want, then choosing a hardwood can potentially give you a more durable and beautiful table. In which case, going straight to a hardwood supplier will be your best option. Generally speaking, smaller independent suppliers will often know more about their own products and how they have been stored and dried, etc. I would recommend making phone calls first, so you can get an idea of the type of wood they supply and the quantities they are used to dealing in. For example, it may be the case that the firm you choose are large and only want to sell substantial volumes of wood. Even if they do sell you the small quantity of wood you require, they may be reluctant to manoeuvre huge stacks of wood with a forklift while you individually pick out a particular length of straight wood with a favourable grain pattern.

Finding a reliable supplier can potentially make a huge difference to how successful your table build will be. If they can give you good information and quality advice about the wood you purchase, this can help you to avoid problems later on down the line. It is always best to be honest and to explain what you are going to be doing with the wood and if you don't understand their jargon or specific terminology then say so. Before you make your preliminary phone calls, it is a good idea to have the necessary information at hand, both in terms of what you will require from them and what they will require from you.

Important things to consider about the wood you purchase are:

The species of the wood

There are hundreds of species of trees, some of which will be more suited to your table than others. Popular choices for table making are Oak, Beech, Birch, Elm, Maple and Ash. Each of these have their own particular properties, varying from species to species such as the tensile strength, the colour and the grain pattern. It is also good to stay open to ideas – you may have a particular wood type in mind, but the timber merchant may have something similar or more suitable in stock.

The origin of the wood

Wood can potentially come from anywhere. For example, Oak grows in many parts of the world and you cannot always presume you are buying a locally sourced tree so it is always worth asking. If the tree has not been felled locally, try to buy sustainably sourced wood that has been legally logged.

Drying method

There are two basic types of drying – air drying and kiln drying (although there are different procedures within these methods). In both cases ask if they have information on how long the wood has dried for, what method was used and what is the current moisture content of the wood. A wood that has not been dried is known as green wood.

Grade of wood

Wood is graded on quality. The grades are based on the number of defects in the wood. Generally speaking, fewer knots or smaller knots and a more uniform colour and grain pattern will signify a higher grade of wood. The higher the grade of wood, the more expensive it will be. In softwoods such as pine, the timber is usually graded for its strength rather than its appearance, whereas hardwoods are often graded on the quantity of clear material that can be obtained.

Machining

Cutting, shaping or preparing your wood is known as machining. Your wood supplier may have machining facilities on site and it may be worth getting your wood cut to size. It may be more expensive, but it could eliminate the need to transport it to a specific wood machinist and it is also going to reduce the waiting time for your timber to be ready to work on.

Cost

The cost of timber obviously varies depending on the species, the quality and the place you are buying from. It is good to have a figure in mind, but you should also consider the amount of time and effort you are going to put in to the project. It can be sensible to spend a little more if it means getting the wood you want.

Delivery

You may not have the facilities to transport large lengths of wood around but don't let this put you off making your own table as most woodyards will have a delivery service. There may be a minimum order to get free delivery, but even if you have to pay, it might not be as much as you think in the grand scheme of things.

Dimensions

Have the dimensions of your table and the component parts at hand. Softwood timber is usually cut in 2in wide intervals (2in, 4in, 6in, 8in) and lengths of 2.4m, 3m, 3.6m, 4.2m and 6m. On the other hand, hardwoods are often cut to whatever width and length the log allows. Be sure to increase the dimensions to give you some room to play with in case some splitting occurs or you need to cut the wood straight again should it twist or warp.

It may also be worth considering reclamation yards to source your wood. It is best to go in person to these places, so you can get a feel for lots of different types of wood and choose one that is suitable for your project. If you do find something you like, you can often pick out the particularly good straight lengths you need at these yards a little more easily than at the large suppliers. The reclamation yards will often also have machines available to cut your wood to the size required, so again make sure you have your cut lists to hand. The staff should be able to tell you about the type of wood and where it has been reclaimed from, but sometimes a wood can be hard to identify. In my experience, you can get some wonderful species of exotic hardwood from places like these that have, for example, been ripped out of old buildings. However, I strongly advise if you are buying these hardwoods from new that you avoid the support of illegal deforestation by buying sustainable wood.

The timber trade is consumer-led just like other products, so buying ethically means you are not supporting illegal deforestation. If you buy sustainable wood, you are supporting forests that are managed to prevent damage to the environment by taking a long-term view of the trees as a resource. If you buy from countries in the EU there is a good chance it is sustainable wood because of the legal measures introduced that protect woodland and forests. EU law limits annual harvesting and has a minimum requirement on replacing harvested trees. Wood from Asia, Africa, South America or even North America comes with fewer guarantees, but the only way to be sure that what you buy comes from well-managed sustainable sources is by looking for the Forestry Stewardship Council (FSC) logo. The FSC is an independent not-for-profit organisation that provides an internationally recognised standard assurance to any business that supports responsible forestry.

The ideal scenario in terms of the environment is to source a tree locally; this also supports your local industries. Recently I clad a shed in London Plane, which was prepared from a tree that had been felled for safety reasons within a mile of the build. I found it a beautiful wood to work with and it gave the shed a personality and a story. It had been quarter sawn stock which gives this particular wood a distinctive and attractive fleck figuring known as lacewood.

If you can buy your wood from a local saw mill you'll also often get a better price because it cuts out the middle man and you will probably be dealing with a person who knows the wood. They may know under what circumstances the tree was felled or may have even felled it themselves (as was true of my Ash tree). They will also know how long it has been seasoning and under what conditions, and they should be able to give you advice on what further steps you may need to take before you commence work.

It is worth adding that wherever you buy your wood, there may be a front of house that is not necessarily representative of the company.

In other words, try not to be put off by a receptionist who doesn't have the information you require, but in such circumstances, ask for one of the sales staff or better still one of the woodworkers or machinists to help you. Finally, regardless of where you have bought your wood and the drying method used, it should always be acclimatised to its environment before work starts. There is nothing worse than putting your heart into a project only to see your carefully constructed table joints ruined as soon as you bring the table indoors (*below*: the lacewood of the London Plane).

Types of wood

Here are some of the more popular types of wood for table making. The types of wood that are readily available will differ depending on where you are in the world. Since I am in Britain, I have included European varieties of tree species for you to consider.

SCOTS PINE *Pinus sylvestris (Pinaceae)*

The genus *Pinus* is made up of evergreen trees that are found in temperate regions in the northern hemisphere. It is the most economically important genus of conifer in the construction trade predominantly because it is a fast-growing softwood that can develop in relatively close stands. There are somewhere in the region of 126 species of pine. A good representative species would be Scots Pine of which a large volume of lumber is produced in Scandinavia. Typically the heartwood is pale reddish-brown and clearly distinct from the paler, creamy white to yellow sapwood. The wood is resinous and knotty, and its texture may be fine or coarse, depending on its origin. All pines have a lot of resin canals. The word 'pine' is in fact derived from Latin *Pinus*, which can be traced to the Indo-European base pit 'resin' (source of English pituitary). The wood is soft, medium in weight and density, with good strength properties. Pine is not a durable wood, and is vulnerable to the weather and to insect attack.

The genus *Betula* contains up to 60 species of trees native to the northern hemisphere. Birch trees can be found as far north as the Arctic and are one of the few species to grow in Iceland and Greenland. The Birch tree features largely in the folklore and culture of Northern European cultures, often symbolising growth and renewal because of its ability to sustain harsh conditions and to repopulate areas damaged by forest fires or clearings. The sapwood is creamy white to pale brown, with little distinction between the sapwood and heartwood. The wood is generally straight grained and of a fine, even texture. It is strong and has a high crushing strength. It dries quite slowly and shrinkage can be substantial so care should be taken. It has little resistance to decay, but takes stain and polishes well, often finishing with an attractive satin sheen.

EUROPEAN BEECH *Fagus sylvatica*

The genus *Fagus* comprises only about ten species. It is often grown as an ornamental shade tree because of its large canopy. Young Beech trees often retain their leaves through autumn and winter and so are frequently used for hedgerows. Beech is an excellent firewood with a bright, prolonged calm flame burning for many hours. Beech wood tablets were a common writing material in Germanic societies before the development of paper. In many languages the word for Beech is similar to that of book. Beech trees can reach 100ft (30m) and sometimes much taller. The Beech is one of the strongest timbers. It is dense and hard with a high crushing strength, but because of its short grain structure it lacks the tensile strength of wood like Ash. The colour is light tan or pale brown although it can darken to a deeper reddish-brown. It has a straight grain with a characteristic fleck. It can take time to season Beech because it is prone to splitting and distortion due to the considerable shrinkage. It is also susceptible to deterioration if left outside. It is perishable and can be vulnerable to the common furniture beetle.

EUROPEAN ASH *Fraxinus excelsior*

The genus *Fraxinus* contains about 70 species, which typically survive for over 200 years and can grow to 20–35m in 45 years. Because of its strength, high shock resistance and straight grain, Ash is often used for striking tools and sports equipment as well as furniture, and traditionally it was used for coach framing and wheelwrighting. The colour is cream to light tan, and the sapwood is not always clearly defined from the heartwood. Ash is tough, resilient with good elasticity and is an excellent wood for steam bending because of its long fibres. It dries fairly quickly, so care is needed to avoid splitting. Since the wood for my table is Ash, I will go into greater detail about this tree later in the book.

EUROPEAN OAK *Quercus robur* and *Quercus petraea*

The genus *Quercus* comprises over 600 species in the northern hemisphere. Of all the wood grown in Northern Europe, Oak has the most historical and cultural significance especially in Britain. There are Oaks that are over 800 years old and it is common for an Oak to live more than 300 years. There is evidence that Oak was used for building over 9,000 years ago and since medieval times Oak has been the principal material for furniture making. The heartwood varies from light tan, to biscuit, to deep brown with distinct bands of earlywood and latewood. The grain is usually straight but cross grain can occur and the wood has appealing grain markings especially when quarter sawn. The wood is fairly hard, heavy and dense with high crushing and bending strength.

It dries slowly and shrinkage is high. Oak trees have a high resistance to insect and fungal attack because of their high tannin content.

DUTCH ELM *Ulmus hollandica*

The genus *Ulmus* comprises up to 60 species of tree. Unfortunately, the world population of Elms has been devastated by the spread of Dutch Elm Disease. Some experimental disease-resistant hybrids have been developed, which could be capable of restoring the Elm back to forestry. The wood of the Elm is a dull brown. It is valued for its interlocking grain and its consequent resistance to splitting, but it also bends and distorts well and was used significantly in wagon wheel hubs, chair seats and boat building. The annual rings are conspicuous because of the large pores in the earlywood. It dries rapidly and can experience distortion unless care is taken. The Elm was popular as a street tree in avenue planting because of its quick growth, tolerance of air pollution and rapid decomposition of foliage. Elm wood is also resistant to decay even when permanently wet. Hollowed trunks were sometimes used as pipes, but resistance to decay does not extend to ground contact and in fact it is prone to rapid rot and decay and thus is a popular coffin wood.

Other popular choices of wood for table making are Maple, Horse Chestnut, Walnut and Cherry, but it is absolutely worth considering any wood that becomes available and with a little research it is possible to find out if a particular wood is suitable.

The wood stack and the right to believe

'Act as if what you do makes a difference ...
it does.'

WILLIAM JAMES

From my original slabs of tree, I now have all the necessary cuts of wood from which to make a table. The next stage is to get this wood dry enough to be able to work with. We decide the best thing for the wood is to stack it and start air drying it outdoors while we try to find a local kiln-drying service. There are many reasons to dry wood before you start to work on it. Dry wood is far stronger than green wood – its stiffness and hardness are increased by up to 50 per cent, it is significantly more resistant to decay, sap stain or mould, and it takes preservatives or polishes better. Dry wood is also lighter in weight, which makes it easier to handle, and over a full day's work of manoeuvring large lengths of wood into position this can make a difference. However, by far the most important reason is when wood is dry its dimensional stability is greater and it is this which will have the most significant effect on the longevity of your table.

My tree had been felled for nearly a year and in this time it had sat on high ground. Although it had been exposed to the rain, there was also a constant, determined wind on the open field where it lay and my hope was that this had aided the drying process. The best time to dry your wood is really dependent on the area you are in. In some cases, it can be a good idea to begin drying in the winter months, so that the process doesn't start too quickly, but generally in terms of drying you will have most success before the weather turns and becomes too damp. Most wood doesn't dry well in very cold winters when the cells can freeze. Similarly little drying can occur if you are in an area where the humidity and rainfall is high in the summer months.

I had very little choice in the matter, but as it happened October was not a bad time.

We decide the best place to stack our wood is outside next to Robbie's workshop. The walls and the roof of the building provide some shelter from the rain, while the open fields either side allow the prevailing wind to blow right through. Airflow is everything when seasoning your timber, so for this reason we stack and separate our wood with stickers. These are sticks, usually a non-staining, neutral batten of around 1–2in^2 multiplied by the width of the stack, so around 90cm for us. These stickers allow circulation between the wood, and without these, many woods will generate fungus or mould. This mould may not affect the wood structurally, but it can permanently stain it. We stack the stickers in a line vertically, so the weight of the wood is transferred through them, which would help to avoid any warping or twisting as it dried.

If the wind is the friend of the drying stack, the rain is the foe. Once we have stacked all of our wood, we cover the top with some corrugated sheets of roofing to protect it from rain and also, to some degree, intense sunlight. Protection from sunlight becomes more important depending on the time of year. In some warmer climates strong, direct sunlight has the potential to dry the wood too quickly and cause checking (end splitting). Finally, we weigh down the stack with some heavy logs, which would keep the sheets of roofing in place, alongside their primary purpose of combatting any warping or cupping of the wood as it dried.

At this juncture in the table-making experience I would say we hit an obstacle, partly due to a lack of knowledge and experience, and partly because drying wood needs time. The obstacle is the difficulty in finding a kiln service. I spend a full two days calling around in search of a company that would be willing to dry my ash, and it proves unexpectedly difficult to find one. Most of the services I find on the internet are large operations and they are not interested in drying such a small amount of timber. I only find one person who has a small kiln marketed towards my situation, which is a vacuum kiln, but this is in Kent and it had been broken for a year. The other services I find online are all in America – a little too far to go for this project. I enquire about adding my timber to a drying load at one of the large companies, but they explain that it doesn't work like that. In order for the timber to be dried correctly, it would need to be of the same wood type and dimensions as the other wood in the kiln. In hindsight, I could have contacted a kiln service and asked what dimensions would be suitable, then had the wood cut again once it was dry.

Still, before the project started, I had expected problems and, to some extent, I had been ready to welcome them. I have read many books in which demonstrations of a particular skill go perfectly and the mishaps are never discussed, but this is seldom realistic. It is useful to understand why obstacles arise so we can learn to avoid them, and how we perceive and react to problems contributes to our ability to overcome them. I could have easily gone out to buy the wood and it would have been more straightforward, but the fact that I had started my table-making project with the tree had already taught me more about wood and carpentry than I could have anticipated. The difficulty in cutting the tree slab with a blunt blade taught me how to sharpen a chainsaw and the oversized slab cuts taught me to find out the limits of my intended saw mill. So, I knew that as long as I reacted in the right way, the difficulties in finding a kiln would teach me more about how to dry wood.

This attitude is partly influenced by my interest in a philosophy that emerged from the United States over the course of the 19th century, known as pragmatism. To me it feels as though in the same way that the pragmatist approach with its practical, utilitarian and independent way of thinking must have been needed to endure the hardships of building a new nation, it is also necessary in carpentry for much the same reasons. William James (1842–1910) followed on from great American thinkers such as Henry David Thoreau, Ralph Waldo Emerson and especially his lifelong friend Charles Sanders Peirce. Central to the pragmatists' beliefs was the theory that we acquire knowledge by doing and not simply by observing. They felt that knowledge should serve a purpose and if it ceases to do so, we add to it or replace it. For James this reasoning was also applicable to the notion of truth. For example, the truth of an idea depends on how useful it is and if an idea can provide a means of predicting something accurately enough for its purpose, then there is no reason not to consider it true. He also stated that truth happens to an idea, that an idea is made true by events and putting an idea into practice is the process by which it comes true.

James thought that having belief was an important element in whether we choose to act upon on idea or not, and when faced with a decision, belief in any course of action will contribute to its success. It would be great if we always had all the information we needed to make a decision, but in life this is not always possible. Either there is not enough time or there is not enough evidence to help us consider and sometimes we have to rely on our belief to drive us into action. James called this 'the right to believe' and he explained it by using the example of a man lost and starving in a forest. The man sees a path; if he believes this is not a way out of the forest then he will stay in the forest and starve, but if he believes that this path will lead him out of the forest then this belief contributes to him making the right decision to follow the path and find his way out. By acting on the idea that the path will save him, it becomes true.

In my experience, I think more deeply when I am confronted with a problem and therefore I know that if I can perceive a problem as a means of learning something, then it can be a good thing. Problems will always arise, but how we react to them is what matters; it is taking part in the process and having a belief in what we can achieve that allows us to learn. So, armed with this sense of belief, Robbie and I set about turning our 'problem' into a solution and we decide to learn more about the drying process and build a kiln for ourselves.

⌐ *Right*: William James

Kiln drying and moisture content

> 'Knowing trees, I understand the meaning
> of patience.'
>
> HAL BORLAND

Most kiln-drying techniques involve introducing heat of some sort to a compartment in which the wood is placed and using non-saturated air to reduce the moisture content within the wood. Drying wood in a heated chamber is effective but can be complex, because of the many variables involved, including the dimensions, the type of wood and the current moisture content of the wood – all of which must be taken into account when calculating drying schedules. Heat is usually circulated in the kiln to keep the temperatures around the wood consistent and to reduce the moisture content, but if care is not taken the wood can dry too fast. For this reason steam is often added to the air, slowing down the drying rate and allowing more control through humidification. Drying can last anywhere from five days to six weeks depending on which process is used and the type of wood and size involved.

There are variations on the kiln-drying process. A vacuum kiln can dry timber in the fastest time and also uses less energy as water boils at a lower temperature in a vacuum. This process is often used for speed and it can also improve the quality of the wood, although they sometimes charge a premium for the service. A solar kiln, which is basically a greenhouse that uses vents or a condensing system, is cheap to run because it uses the sun's energy but it is slower and less predictable.

The type of kiln I decide to build is a form of dehumidification kiln. This variation is based on the principle of placing the wood in a sealed chamber to reduce the moisture content of the air and thereby reduce the

moisture content of the wood. When we talk of wood being dry, we are really describing the wood as being dry enough to become stable for its purposes. In fact, all wood (including dry wood) still contains moisture; the amount of moisture in wood is measured as a percentage of the weight when completely dry. This percentage can range from anywhere between 40 per cent and 200 per cent; a piece of wood with a moisture content of 200 per cent means that twice as much of its weight is due to water as wood.

By now, my stack had been in the brisk Derbyshire wind for about a month and at this point we want to get an idea of the current moisture content. The easiest way to achieve this is to buy a moisture meter. A good moisture meter can be quite expensive, but if you are involved in furniture making then it is an essential piece of kit. The moisture meters used by professionals are usually the meters that incorporate two pads which transmit and receive a signal when pressed against the wood. These are non-evasive and require only a surface contact to obtain a reading. However, you can buy a relatively cheap one for around £20, which was going to be adequate for my purposes. These more basic types consist of two pins which measure the electrical resistance of the wood. Since water freely conducts electricity, increasing water content correlates to increased conductance. In order to get a true reading, you need to push these pin electrodes into the wood fibres, which can sometimes leave marks on the wood surface, but since my wood was in its rough sawn state this didn't present a problem.

Upon taking the readings of my wood in the stack, rather surprisingly the moisture content had already reduced to between 22 per cent and 30 per cent. On the face of it this was good news, as I had expected the water content to be higher. The amount of water a tree contains when it has been recently felled varies from species to species, but in most cases is around 50 per cent moisture content. Generally, Elm comes in at 58 per cent, Oak and Beech at 47 per cent, and Birch at 43 per cent. The moisture content of Ash is relatively low compared with other species at around 33 per cent. Air drying will usually only reduce the moisture content to between 15 per cent and 20 per cent, and taking into consideration the Derbyshire autumn climate, I would have only expected my wood to reduce to around the 20 per cent mark anyway, so we felt the sooner we could get the wood in our kiln the better.

The first step is to move the stack from outside and set it up on a bench in the workshop, as our idea was to build a kiln around this new stack. We follow similar principles as the first time, basically stacking it in much the same position as it had lain as a tree on the top of that windswept field. As we dismantle the stack, we notice the wood has begun to warp a little on the lengths, so in an attempt to reduce this as much as we could, we strap the wood tightly together.

We paint the end grains of the wood with a 50/50 mix of PVA glue and water, which should really have been done as soon as the wood was first cut. Water evaporates out of the surface of wood, then the moisture deeper within the wood gets drawn out towards the surface. The ends

are sealed to retard the process because moisture escapes from the ends of the wood about 10–12 times faster than the other surfaces and wood that dries too quickly is more prone to checking and end graining. Next, we construct a basic frame made from 2in x 1in battens around the stack of wood. The frame is built in two halves; the lower half is just shy of the top of the stack, the upper half acts like a lid. The reason for this is that we still want to weigh down the wood, so the lid needs to be in contact with the stack. The weight would help to prevent warping and, in particular, cupping as the moisture left the wood.

We wrap the frame of the wood in polyurethane plastic sheeting, taking care not to leave any gaps so it creates an airtight chamber. We leave access to it from one end so we can put the dehumidifier inside and also so we can periodically monitor the moisture levels of our wood stack. The aim of this whole process is to reduce the moisture content of the wood to as close to 10 per cent as possible. Once reduced to this lower moisture content, the stability of the wood would become predictable enough to work with and we would have a greater confidence that the joints would not expand or contract too much. However, given the circumstances of drying the wood at a reasonably cold and damp time of year and with the added unpredictability of using a homemade kiln, the results are far from certain. It is also worth mentioning that a piece of wood that has been reduced to 10 per cent moisture content will not necessary stay that way. Wood will always have the ability to absorb moisture, known as moisture pick-up because wood is a hygroscopic material, meaning that it wants to reach a state of equilibrium with the air that surrounds it. In fact, how dry a piece of wood needs to be really depends on the environment it will ultimately be used in.

Once the dehumidifier is in place, we fit a hose, which would remove the water without having to open the sealed chamber we had made. We also place an electric fan into the chamber to keep the air flowing. This would help to keep the drying consistent over all the surfaces of wood. Then it is just a case of being patient and crossing our fingers that the wood would dry in time to make our table.

Tools: our first and last connection

'We shape our tools and afterwards our tools shape us.'

MARSHALL McLUHAN

At the heart of the philosophy surrounding all traditional crafts, you will find the concept of 'connection', and the first and last connection in table making is with your tools. Carpentry is not possible without tools. After all, they allow us to manipulate wood into the various shapes and dimensions we require to make an object. Tools have both a physical and a conceptual power because they connect our human imagination to physical forms, by making it possible to bring into existence the increasingly complex ideas in our minds.

Tools and work take a journey together; they co-evolve. Just as the tool shapes the wood, the wood informs the toolmaker how to shape the tool in return. Although wood is a highly complex material, it lends itself to manipulation through tools. From one perspective wood is a hard, rigid material that we could never alter with our hands, but once we involve very simple tools, wood becomes a soft material, malleable, easy to cut, split, shave and file into any shape or form. The relationship between a tool and the work it produces is the history of all tools, but it is especially interesting in carpentry because it goes right back to the beginnings of making and therefore has had a great deal of influence on what it is to be human.

The type of tools you use and the way in which you use them will determine whether your table will be a good or a bad one. Knowledge is seldom enough in life, and never enough in carpentry. You have to take the knowledge which exists in your mind and put it into your hands or it is useless. You cannot use words to disguise how proficient you are in the way that you might be able to get away with in some professions – in carpentry you are judged solely on the work that is produced and that is why woodwork is so honest. In the past, a carpenter would have made their own toolbox and saw stools as a way to show off their prowess as a woodworker. This tradition may have gone now, but the judgemental glance from fellow workers will still assess how ordered your toolkit is or how sharp your chisels are, and for good reason. The respect you give to your tools says something about you as a carpenter and as a person.

It still baffles me to see cheap tape measures, unthreatening knives or rusty old saws labouring their way through a work day. By caring for your tools you are displaying a respect for the time you will spend working and therefore a respect for your way of life. It can take time piecing together hand tools that you are happy with and your toolkit will inevitably evolve as your work progresses. Whether you enjoy buying vintage tools from car boot sales or you have a set of expensive brand-new tools, the most important thing is to use them relentlessly until they become familiar to the hand. The aim is to master the movements until the hand positions and the forces involved become instinctive. Working well with a tool depends as much on the skills of the carpenter as it does on how well the tool is set up and how familiar the tool is.

For example, when I pick up my hand plane and slice a paper-thin layer of wood from my table top, it is with a single controlled movement that I do so, but behind this action, beneath the surface, is a multitude of connecting elements. The wood is stripped cleanly because the plane is set up correctly. The foot is level and flat; the pitch angle of the cutting iron is low enough to split the fibres in front of the cutting edge but steep enough to prevent the grain tearing out; the back iron is tight to prevent chattering; the mouth aperture is open just enough to allow the wood to escape and the blade is sharpened to a standard that I would happily shave with. If the machine is tuned and working well, I know what it is capable of because I have trained my body to understand it. I can hear the high-pitched hissing noise as it glides across the surface of the wood and leaves a long silky shaving in its path. I know how to transfer my weight rhythmically to create a smooth action because I have repeated the movement over and over until it becomes second nature, and because I know the plane. I feel relaxed and I am able to work in the present moment and focus on one action alone.

Hand tools

The following hand tools are the ones which will be most useful for the purposes of making a table and most of them we will use on this project.

Handsaw

We use different saws in carpentry depending on the cut required as this will affect the shape and size of the saw as well as the blade design. The two most useful saws for table making are a cross-cut saw and a tenon saw. The cross-cut saw is used for cutting across the grain of the wood. It has tapered teeth on the forward and trailing edges designed for the job, but a regular disposable handsaw will usually have a similar blade design and will be good enough for the purposes of this job. The tenon saw is not surprisingly going to be used to make your tenon cuts. It is in many ways a thinner, smaller version of a cross-cut saw, but with much finer teeth to achieve a more accurate cut. It often has a brass top plate to keep it stiff and perfectly straight when cutting. You can pick old-fashioned ones up quite easily, as a seller will often consider the saw to be past its best because it is blunt, but it is relatively straightforward to get it sharpened. Buying one second hand, even with the cost of sharpening, can be cheaper than buying new and there is a good chance it will be a superior tool because of the better manufacturing techniques used to make old tools.

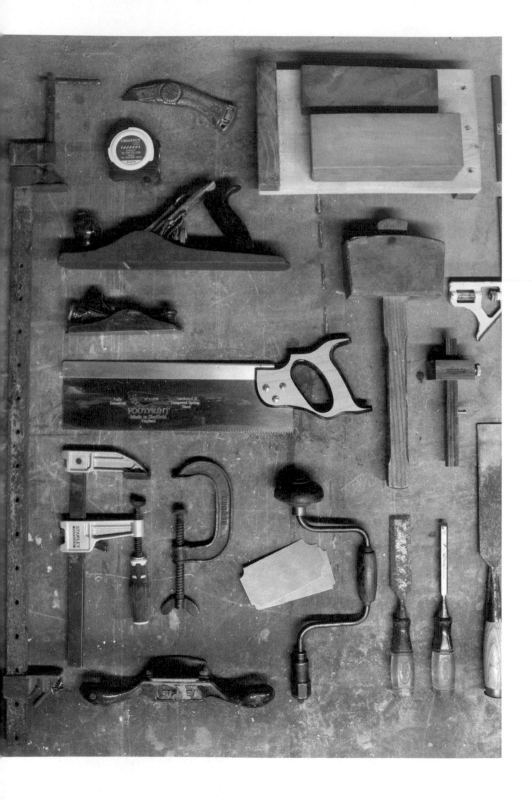

The chisel is arguably the most versatile and essential of the carpenter's tools. The quality, razor-sharp chisel is revered by your fellow workers, while the rusty, blunt chisel is ridiculed. There are hundreds of chisels, each coming in a variety of shapes and sizes with a wide range of handles. For the purposes of table making, the most useful is a mortise chisel. A mortise chisel has a square, steel blade, sharpened at the front and with square edges. Mortises are square and so a square chisel is fit for purpose, as the square edge makes the chisel more durable because there is more steel and it is easier to sharpen. Again mortise chisels can often be purchased second hand and, if blunt, sharpening will easily bring them back to life. A more general-purpose chisel is known as a bevelled chisel because it has bevelled edges on the sides. This type of chisel is more flexible because it can reach smaller areas and create angles which can be useful when, for example, you are making dovetails. The vast majority of modern chisels are now bevelled chisels and this type will do the job just fine if you cannot find a mortise chisel. In terms of sizes it is useful to have a basic set which usually consists of ¼in, ½in, ¾in and 1in, and this range can handle most jobs. For table making, a mortise would usually be a third the thickness of the timber you are using, which is why a set is good so you can simply choose the chisel size that is most suitable. It is also useful to have a wide chisel for cleaning up your tenons, because a wide chisel means you are not digging into the wood and having to do the same movement multiple times. Chisels should be sharpened to around 30 degrees, but this can be altered slightly higher or lower with experience depending on your technique or what you are hoping to achieve. The sharper your chisel the less force will be required to cut into the wood fibres, making for better quality work. This razor-sharp edge makes the chisel deceptively one of the most dangerous tools and you can easily slice open your skin if you use it carelessly. The basic rules to avoid this are: do not hold on to the wood with one hand and hold the chisel in the other and always work away from any body part.

Hand Drill

In the building trade, hand drills have largely been replaced by the portable power drill in its various forms, but like many of the simple hand tools, we should not forget just how good they can be at accomplishing the task they were designed for. The hand drill can be more accurate at times because of the slow pace at which you can turn it. Again, markets and car boot sales are ideal for picking up these little gems, largely because people consider them

to be ornaments now due to the advancement of the modern power tool. If you do intend to use a hand drill, there are two basic types – the brace and bit drill and a small egg beater-type drill. The brace and bit drill is used for making the larger holes required for drilling out mortises. This drill has more leverage and therefore more torque than the smaller egg beater-type, which is really only useful for drilling small holes. The brace and bit drill usually has a chuck that receives round and small drill bits, although the bits with the round shanks tend to twist in the chuck more easily. These hand drills can often take a larger drill bit than many of the powered drills. When it comes to drill bits, an auger bit is the most commonly used for the mortise. A standard twist bit may be helpful if you are going to use a dowel to hold the tenon in place or to dowel the table top together.

Mallet

The use of a hammer in furniture making is generally quite rare. In most cases it is a small, light hammer of around 4 to 6 ounces for driving in fine pins or brads. The most common striking tools for table making are a mallet or a rubber hammer. If you manage to get a good quality, well-balanced mallet, the transfer of energy can make it a surprisingly enjoyable and powerful tool to use. A steel hammer should never be used to drive a chisel because it could damage the chisel; a wooden mallet is best usually made from one of the softer hardwoods, such as Beech or Ash with a handle made from an impact-resistant timber, such as Hickory or Ash. I know some carpenters that use a favourite battered old piece of wood that they have had for years because they have grown fond of it; it really depends what you are used to. A rubber mallet can be useful for assembling joints, as it will avoid any unsightly dents in your beautifully worked timber.

Clamp

Sash clamps or bar clamps are used to apply pressure when gluing the table top together and for assembling the table base. You need to obtain clamps of a greater width than your table in order to keep it together. A decent sash clamp generally consists of a long bar of steel with a tommy bar at one end to tighten a screw-operated jaw, and on the other end an adjustable jaw is secured with a pin that can be inserted into holes in the bar. The clamp is sometimes a forgotten tool in the workshop, but it is difficult to make any sizeable object without it. A quick-release clamp may also be of use to hold certain pieces in position while work is being carried out.

Square

The steel square is an essential and precise piece of equipment, capable of accurate work. It is used primarily for measuring and marking right angles as well as checking for 'squareness'. Even a wooden built square is useful for large-scale squaring, but if you build one yourself it should be checked for accuracy regularly as they tend to go out with use. For table making, a sliding mitre square or combination square will work the best. The latter is so called because it uses a combination of 45 degrees and 90 degrees. It consists of an adjustable ruler that slides through a stock and is held in place by a spring-loaded locking device. It is a versatile tool and can be used as a depth gauge, a straight edge, a ruler and a marking gauge. A word of warning: if you buy an old one, the second-hand ones are sometimes not square, but there's a quick and easy way to check it before you purchase by simply drawing the angle onto a piece of wood and then turning the square over and drawing it again, if they are the same then it is square and your purchase will be a good one.

Mortise Gauge

The mortise gauge is an adjustable tool that transfers precise measurements onto wood; it is indispensable when marking out joints. It consists of a stem with one spike on one side and two spikes on the other, one of which is adjustable; an adjustable stock is attached to the stem with a locking device. The adjustable widths of the spikes are for marking the size of the mortise or tenon you wish to make. If you are buying a second-hand one, make sure all the parts are present and are still adjustable. Also be sure to check whether they can be tightened up and locked. Other useful tools for marking are a knife, a pencil and, occasionally, a bradawl. I use a quick-release Stanley® knife because it has a stiff blade which is easy to replace if it goes blunt. A knife is also useful to keep your pencil nice and sharp. I will often mark with a knife then use a hard 2H finely sharpened pencil to draw on the knife mark so I can see it properly. The time a bradawl might be useful is as a starting point for drilling holes.

Tape Measure

The tape measure I use for table making is a Stanley® FATMAX 5m – it is wide enough to be rigid and strong, which makes it easier to use. The most common tape lengths are 3m, 5m, 8m and 10m – for table making any size will be enough. It is also useful to have both imperial and metric measurements on your tape because the units of measurements often change in carpentry and it makes it easier to convert them. Use the end hook of a tape if the measurement doesn't need to be perfectly accurate. However, if accuracy is needed then either use the rule on your combination square or measure from 100mm on your tape and deduct this from the reading.

The plane is used to smooth, shape, flatten or reduce the thickness of wood. The sole of the plane glides over the surface of your wood and an angled blade shaves the surface – the thickness of this shaving can be controlled by adjusting the blade position. For table making the two main types of planes that are most useful are the jack plane and the block plane. The jack plane is used primarily as a way of getting your wood surfaces level. For example, if you have constructed your table carcass and there is a little waviness in your apron, then the jack plane can be used to straighten it out. They are around 14in or 15in long and the blade is usually fixed at an angle of around 45 degrees, with the bevel facing downwards. Technically a jointer plane would be used for table surfacing but these are often over 24in long, so a jack plane is going to be easier and cheaper to purchase. Block planes are usually 6in long and are a very versatile tool as they can be set to a lower angle than the jack plane and can be used with one hand. The block plane is one of the most useful tools in the workshop – it is good for cutting end grain, for chamfering edges and for surfacing. However, if you try to get a table level with a block plane, its short length will mean that the plane follows the contour of the wood and you will not solve the problem. It is imperative you keep the blade on your planes nice and sharp or they will not yield good results. To keep planes in good working order, you can rub the sole with an abrasive block and apply camellia oil. To avoid damaging the sole, try to store it on its side or with one end raised.

Sharpening Stone

All good woodwork involves keeping the blades of your tools razor sharp and the sharpening stone is an absolute necessity if you want your work to be of good quality. There are many different types of stones available, made from either natural or synthetic materials. The two main types you will come across are oil stones and water stones. As the name suggests, you will use oil to lubricate an oil stone and water to lubricate a water stone. The oil stones are a great deal cheaper and will do a good job for the money. They will usually be double sided and have a rough side and smooth side so you only need to buy one stone. An oil stone will wear down much faster than a water stone, so you will see people moving their blade around the stone in an attempt to wear the stone down evenly. Having a water stone means you can just move your blade up and down in a straight line, which makes sharpening easier. You can also buy a diamond stone, which is used dry and is coated with diamond grit, but these are more expensive again. To help you keep the correct angle on your blades you can use a honing guide, which will also preserve a blade's bevelled edge and since it will mean less sharpening it will increase the blade's lifespan. You should always wash your hands after sharpening your tools to avoid marking your wood with dirty fingerprints, especially with oil stone sharpening.

Cabinet Scraper

This is a simple, thin, flat piece of sharp tempered steel, which is used to remove fine shavings from the surface of timber. There are many different types on the market and they will all work well if properly sharpened. For table making, a standard rectangle will be fine to work on the flat surfaces. If your scraper produces dust instead of shavings when drawn across the timber, then it needs to be sharpened. A properly shaped scraper can do wondrous things with wood. It is good to have a couple on the go, so you can keep working should the scraper become blunt and this also means you can sharpen them together.

Power tools

Many of the processes that go into making a table have not changed for hundreds of years and often hand tools are still the most accurate way of completing a task. However, there are undoubtedly a handful of machines that have proved an invaluable addition to the table maker's arsenal. There are some incredible old machines, as we saw in Pete's workshop, but it can be a skill in itself to keep them running. When it comes to industrial purchases then more often than not a brand-new tool is going to be more advanced and more

trustworthy. Generally speaking, you get what you pay for with power tools, so it is wise to consider your purchases carefully. Top-end companies, such as Fez Tools and Mafell, will give you the best chance of accomplishing good work, but many models will overlap with mid- to high-range brands. Of these popular brands, DeWalt, Makita, Bosch, Hilti and Hitachi have a good reputation for mass-producing quality and robust tools.

Borrowing tools or buying second hand is risky, because not being aware of a tool's particular quirk means you cannot predict its actions, and saving on a new purchase is never going to be worth an injury. Do not just walk into your nearest shop and choose the first tool that you believe will do the job – my advice is to buy the best tool that you can afford. You should do the necessary research, read through the reviews and when you think you have made your choice, find a shop that stocks it and take a look at it to see if it has everything you had expected – hold it in your hand and check the balance. After all, how often do you buy nice things for yourself? You should enjoy the experience and savour the moment.

Here is a list of the powered tools which are most beneficial to the table maker, many of which have become standard in the workshop.

Chop Saw

The chop saw or sliding mitre saw is a versatile machine that will be used constantly in a workshop because of its speed and accuracy. These saws are incredibly useful for mitre cuts, but in terms of table making, the benefit of having one is basically going to be the speed at which you can cut all the required timber to the correct length. It is not an expensive tool in comparison to some power tools. I use a DeWalt mitre saw, but of all the power tools, some of the cheaper chop saws can work reasonably well. Perhaps this is because the saw is fixed so it doesn't lose accuracy. It is sensible to screw down your chop saw and make sure it is stable, as people often forget to do this. It is also worth buying the rollers, which can be placed either end of your bench to support the long lengths of wood, so you don't require an extra pair of hands. As with all power tools, the chop saw is dangerous and you need to focus; avoid the common but monumental error of chopping off the end of your thumb on the hand that holds the wood as you look at the pencil mark you have just made!

Table Saw

If you've got the space and you can afford it, the table saw is the other workhorse in a workshop. It can save countless hours. We used a Metabo to cut down our

tree slabs into boards. Although this is a good saw, it is built for transporting to site work, so there is a lot of plastic in it to make it light enough to carry around. For the same money you could get a heavier, but more powerful one. A sawdust extractor is a good addition to the workshop if you can manage to get hold of one, as the open blade puts a lot of dust into the air. With the table saw, the blade is often on show, so it is imperative to be careful around one of these machines. The blade guard and rip fence are there to help protect you, but don't get lulled into a false sense of security. You should research how to use one properly. As always, the best safety device is a good operator.

Sander

Sanders are used to level and smooth a surface in preparation for the final finish. The modern sanders have made the laborious task of sanding a relatively quick and easy procedure. Before the powered sander, carpenters would have hand planed each component part to exact dimensions prior to assembly, but these days it is more common to finish a table to rougher dimensions and then level and smooth the table once assembly is complete. There are two main types of sander that can be used on a table. The belt sander is generally used first because of its ability to sand large areas of wood quickly. It consists of two rollers to which a belt of sandpaper is attached. Take care and do not rush the belt sander, as they can remove wood aggressively. The random orbit sander is often more of a finishing sander, although it can also sand large areas quickly. The sandpaper is usually held in place with a Velcro pad. This sander is more suited to a smoother sandpaper than the belt sander and can be used for polishing.

Surface Planer and Thicknesser

The surface planer and thicknesser allow you to produce flat, square pieces of timber sections – a basic requirement for table making. They will often have two settings: the planer can be used to smooth faces and edges and the thicknesser will produce sections of uniform thickness. Regularising a piece of timber without a thicknesser takes skill and time, so it is a really useful piece of kit, but it is also a substantial piece of equipment and it is common for the amateur carpenter go to a workshop to do this stage. If you are serious about your carpentry work and you do wish to purchase one, they make smaller, more portable ones, if space is a concern.

Bench Grinder

The bench grinder has become an essential piece of kit in the workshop for re-sharpening all the blades on your various tools – it is so cheap these days that there is no reason why you wouldn't have one to save time. If you are using a sharpening stone and you are not an experienced sharpener then after a while your chisels can start to lose their shape. The bench grinder is especially useful for starting again, as you can grind them quickly back to straight then return to your sharpening stone with more confidence. If you pay a little more to get different speed settings, it can be easier to control and it is also advisable to get two wheels – one arbour with a coarse stone for rough sharpening and the other with some kind of smooth stone for high-speed sharpening or polishing. You can also buy grinders with water cooling to prevent your stone from overheating, which will preserve the temper of your blade.

These are the power tools I consider to be the most effective for making a table, but there will be others. It really depends how much you want to do by hand and how much space you have at your disposal. Of the other power tools on the market you could consider a drill driver for drilling out your mortises and dowels, a portable circular saw if you don't have room for a chop saw, a router for different kinds of edge finishing, biscuit jointers for joining your table tops together and mortises for making your joints.

A note on safety, because all power tools are dangerous. Don't use faulty or damaged power tools and always keep your work area tidy. Try to put good practice into your body right from the start, as being well balanced will help with all tools and it will increase your ability to react in the right way should something go wrong, for example, when a machine kicks back. Tool quality, maintenance and technique are factors in working safely, but by far the most important aspect is in your mind. Most injuries I have seen on site are either from people rushing or from people who have used power tools their whole lives and have just become complacent. I tell my workers to pause for a split second before using any power tool – this may not sound like much, but I find it just gives you the space to be aware and to focus. Understanding the danger of a tool allows you to adjust your behaviour, but you should not be in fear of a power tool, as this will not help you. Anxieties will transfer through your body in the form of tension. When approaching a power tool, it is more a case of respect; remember a quality power tool is a wonderful thing – be good to your power tools and they will make your life easier.

Part 2
The Table Top

'Kogei' and the art of craft

'The highest reward for a person's toil is not what he gets for it, but what he becomes by it.'

JOHN RUSKIN

In life it is good to understand different perspectives, to be open and able to work in new ways, to read not just one book, but many books in order to understand a subject. Life is richer if we teach ourselves to think like another person or to imagine what it might feel like to be another creature or even an object. Of course we shouldn't always believe everything we see. In fact, understanding another's viewpoint can make us feel more strongly about our own, but being open is always beneficial because it expands our field of vision.

At times I take an interest in the Japanese perspective of craftwork, mainly because their traditions are often routed in nature, but also because Japan is traditionally very good at making objects. The Japanese word '*kogei*' captures something of the spirit of this perspective. '*Kogei*' is often translated into English as the word 'craft', but this translation is not sufficient to convey its meaning. Such is the nature of translation – a subtlety in meaning is often lost without its cultural or historical backdrop. The insufficient translation of '*kogei*' into English perhaps says something about the way we have perceived crafts in recent times. In Japan, the word is similar to craft in that it describes the production of utilitarian objects, but a work produced by '*kogei*' is considered both a piece of art and a manufactured product.

In some respects, '*kogei*' draws parallels with the Arts and Crafts movement of the late 19th and early 20th centuries – a movement founded in response to the Industrial Revolution which replaced craft industries with machine-based manufacturing. The philosophical foundation for the Arts

and Crafts movement was built by the arts critic and social thinker John Ruskin, but its leader was to be William Morris, who became well known for his textile designs.

As well as reacting to the negative aesthetic qualities of the Industrial Revolution, the Arts and Crafts movement also opposed the demeaning conditions under which things were made. It sought to return to a simple, more fulfilling way of living. Both Morris and Ruskin believed that if a person could learn to produce work of quality, then the character of the individual producing that work would be improved and hence society would also be improved.

Our working existence and the objects we produce are still largely influenced by the Industrial Revolution, a revolution which was inevitable and perhaps necessary. Machines have made production more efficient and more affordable to some, but because these methods are driven by economic incentives, they have also continued to slowly erode our relationship to craft. The semi-consumable product has disconnected us from our everyday objects, and as a result good craftsmanship has become undervalued.

It is certainly the case that the machines have become expert at the jobs they are designed to do. The machines of the Industrial Revolution began by imitating the hand of the maker, but eventually became so good and so cost effective that the workers no longer needed these original skills. In some cases, the skill of the craftsperson no longer matches the precision work or mathematical accuracy of a machine, but there is more to craft than mathematical accuracy.

An important part of both 'kogei' and the Arts and Craft movement is an understanding of the essence of the material involved. In 'kogei', the material comes first and the techniques that develop to fashion the object are not so much choices to be made, but instead they arise from the result of understanding the nature of the material. The intimacy with which the craftsperson interacts with the material leads to an amalgamation of skill and self-expression that a machine cannot match.

It is also worth remembering that it is not just the maker who has a relationship to the object but the user. A handmade object has a dimension that is favourable to us – it is favourable because the hand that has made it is similar to the hand that will use it. To be able to see the work of this hand awakens our affection, so it feels warmer and it makes us care more about the object. Life is better when we care about it.

I would like to make my own perspective on these matters clear. You can quite easily go out and purchase a functioning table for less money than it will cost you to purchase the materials and tools needed to make the table I am teaching you to make. However, this project is not about money. When we reduce the things we care about in life to their economic value then life loses its meaning. You can also go out and buy a well-made, second-hand table and have it in your dining room this evening. From this table you can certainly learn of the intrinsic value of a table, but this project is not just about having nice things either. To truly understand anything in life you need to get involved, you need to take a step into the unknown, you need to be a part of all aspects of a subject, to work your way through the difficult moments and to experience the joy of succeeding. This is how we learn the true value of things.

Left: William Morris

Right: Jon Ruskin

Preparing your timber

> 'Before anything else, preparation is the key to success.'

ALEXANDER GRAHAM BELL

On a cold early morning in January we set out to turn our tree wood into useable prepared timber. It is still dark as we open up and embark on the ritualistic straightening up of the workshop. A brisk northern wind accompanies the freezing winter temperatures. Within minutes, the weather is biting at our exposed hands, and as we clear some logs outside the workshop it feels as though we are working in a Bruegel painting. Finally the sun peers over the bank of pines to the east and as it does, a flock of 20 or so fieldfare pass by, just out of reach over our heads, the low dawn light catching their cream underbellies and painting them with golden flecks. I had never seen a flock of fieldfare before and just this simple moment immediately hushed the wind and mellowed the cold.

Once the workshop area is straight, we begin to dismantle our homemade dehumidifying kiln to reveal the wood. I feel quite nervous, because more than anything else, the condition of my timber will have a direct bearing on the success or failure of the whole table-making project. As well as the plastic wrapping, we had eventually also covered the kiln with blankets to combat the cold winter temperatures, and as we dismantle we can feel the warmth inside which bodes well for the drying. There is a substantial amount of water in the draining bucket of the dehumidifier, but this could be moisture taken out from the air. In terms of time, it would have been difficult to have done much more. I had left the wood in the kiln for as long as I could, but it was time to make a table.

After dismantling is complete, I check the moisture content and with relief I find the wood is consistently around 12 per cent throughout. There is a little bit of cracking or checking at the end grain closest to the dehumidifier of one board and one of the thinner lengths has bent completely out of shape, but we had purposely cut spare wood from the tree, so we could lose wood in this sort of eventuality. The majority of the wood looks to have escaped any serious warping or twisting and we separate it into two piles – that of table-top wood and table-structure wood. Today we would work on the table-top wood.

Hand planing

Most of the work would be done with the surface planer and thicknesser, but before these power tools became commonplace, the job of making wood even and square would have been done by hand using a plane. I wanted to prepare at least one board this way so I could experience and understand the difficulties.

The first job is to cut the boards to length, and since the drying process has caused a small amount of splitting at the edges of one of the boards, we cut this off with the chop saw and then cut all the other boards the same length. There is no point putting work into any timber that would not be used. Next we plane the face side of the board, which is often the best surface, and then the edge which is at 90 degrees and adjacent to the face side.

The correct tool for this is a large plane called a No. 7 or a jointer plane, which is usually 550mm long and weighs about 4.5kg (10lb). The long foot of the plane produces a straighter edge because it stops the plane from just following any contours in the wood. These planes are quite specialist and can be expensive. The common plane to have in any workshop is the shorter jack plane or No. 5½. It usually measures around 380mm in length – this will be fine for the job and this is the plane I will use. A block plane would not be suitable as it is simply too short to get the edge straight enough.

Planing down a length of wood to prepare it for being glued together sounds simple enough, but it is in fact quite a skilled and labour-intensive job that can take time to master. As always it is best to start by checking the plane. The blade should be sharpened usually to 25 degrees, with the mouth aperture open just enough to let wood escape. The blade should be level and flat with the foot.

The trick with many hand tools is to get a smooth flow going. Using a plane is a similar principle to using a saw – you should try not to force it,

the aim is to let the blade do the work. The back handle should be used for pushing and try not to push down on the front handle especially at the end of the stroke to avoid rounding over the ends of wood. The plane should travel in the same direction as the grain lines, with a slight angle to the direction it is pushed (a shearing angle). If the grain tears, check the blade position or try working from the opposite end.

To monitor the progress of your work, a straight edge is periodically placed on the face or the edge you are working on. Gradually the light that shines between the straight edge and the wood will reduce until the wood corresponds exactly. A square is also used continually to check that the wood is perfectly flat throughout and that the face is at a right angle to the edge. You can also place two sticks (winding sticks) at either end of the length of wood to help you discern if the wood has been planed straight – if the sticks are parallel then the wood is flat. These procedures are repeated until both faces are perfectly parallel and at right angles to the adjacent edges.

The whole process takes me over an hour, my technique gradually improving as my body remembers the rhythms and coordination needed to achieve efficiency of movement, but with more practice it should take a shorter period of time. Planing large volumes of wood is hard work by hand, which explains the introduction of powered workshop tools, but it certainly helps to warm my body and get the blood flowing.

Machine planing

To save time and effort, we prepare the rest of the wood with the surface planer and thicknesser. To save space, these workshop tools are often part of the same machine with the plane on the upper surface and the thicknesser within. The process is largely the same as when preparing timber by hand, so again we plane the face side of the wood, and then the edge.

Our machine is not large but it is enough to do the job. We start by placing the concave surface of the timbers downwards and passing them over the surface plane blade. This avoids the blade just following the contours of the wood. As the wood is pushed through the machine, the plane takes away the high spots usually at the beginning and the end of the pass. As the surface becomes straighter, the noise of the blade planing will become more consistent until finally the machine will plane the full length of board at which point it should be straight. However, again you will need to check the board with a straight edge to ensure the reality fits the theory. We use the same process to get the face side straight. Once we are happy we mark the wood with the standard face-side symbol. Although at this point it was

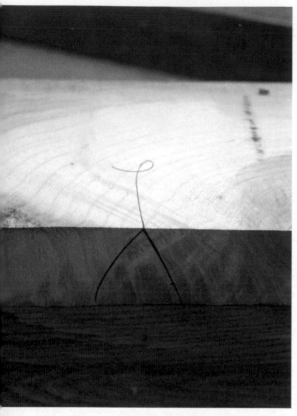

easy to see which surfaces have been planed, as the process continues it will become less obvious, so these marks will help to organise us as the boards are moved around the workshop.

Once we are happy with our face and edge, the next step is to use the thicknesser to get the remaining surfaces square and parallel. The maximum width that can be passed through our thicknesser is 140mm, which I hadn't expected. But carpentry is not an exact science – wood warps, it changes shape, it can split or twist, or machines vary. It is therefore quite common to have to adjust to certain scenarios. In our case, although the boards are to be cut narrower than I had expected, we have enough wood to add another board to ensure the final table is wide enough.

Since we have a table saw in the workshop, we decide to cut all the boards to 140mm before passing them through the thicknesser. This has the added benefit of getting the boards reasonably straight which will minimise the work needed for the thicknesser. A slow steady action is best with all power tools, but especially with a table saw to avoid the blade burning the surface of the wood. We now have six boards ready for the thicknesser. We set the depth to plane just 1.5mm off the remaining surface, though a heavier duty machine would be able to plane more wood with each pass thereby making it faster.

My tree wood is gradually being transformed into workable timber and at this point the process starts to make an impact on me. Robbie feeds the boards through one end of the thicknesser and I receive them at the other end. With each pass, more and more of the wood grain is revealed and my hand is involuntarily drawn to brushing away the sawdust from the new surface to see its beauty. The difference between a rough piece of timber and a planed piece is something akin to peering into the choppy, rippled surface of a lake or the clear, glass view of calm waters.

We continue the passes for the next few hours until we achieve a consistent thickness throughout, so all the faces are parallel and all the edges are square. Our tree wood now looks like the prepared timber that you can buy from a timber merchant, but I am happy that I can still see the various inconsistencies of knot and grain and discolouration. The story of the tree is encased inside the wood and the more I could see of it, the more the tree would remain and hopefully the more connected I would feel to the table.

The day has been a long one, so we stack the wood and once again look forward to getting out of the cold. For me especially, it has been worth the time and effort of preparing the wood ourselves. Taking part in the transformative process and seeing the new wood emerge from the machine has been a memorable experience. We couldn't resist taking a little linseed oil and rubbing it over the smooth surface of the wood to see what the patterns might eventually look like.

There is peace in the workshop rituals

'The disciplined man masters thoughts by
stillness and emotions by calmness.'

LAO-TZU

Constructing a table requires knowledge of the skills needed to make the component parts and fit them together. It also requires the tools to make these component parts and knowledge of how to use them, but this is still not enough. To make a table of quality that will stand the test of time requires an understanding of the rituals involved in making, rituals that help to focus the mind and make the skills possible. Over the years, I have taught myself to associate my workplace with a suitable frame of mind. Being able to calm my thoughts has been especially useful on the days that I don't feel good, either about my work or more generally. We all get these days, depending on what is happening in our personal life or what is happening in the world, but it is my workshop and rituals which drag me back to the land of the living.

The workshop is a special place. I think differently inside its affable walls and as such it has a kind of magic, like the forest itself. Its basic functionality is an antidote to the endless barrage of modernity, whether it is yet another looming economic crisis, or the ineptitude of career politicians to combat climate change, or just the spirit-crushing tasks of everyday existence. The workshop acts as a sanctuary, a place to be closer to a time that existed before modern life, a means to be closer to ourselves. There was, of course, always a modern world advancing towards a future beyond our natural state, and a sanctuary to experience the simple, more meaningful things in life is no new phenomenon.

The American philosopher Henry David Thoreau captures something of this outlook in his book *Walden*, first published in 1854. Part memoir, part spiritual quest, it details the experience of living and working in a cabin (*below*) called 'Walden' in Massachusetts. In *Walden*, Thoreau meditates on the pleasures of escaping society and reflects on the benefits of being closer to nature where time feels more as if it is ours. I will on occasion browse through *Walden* to get myself in the right frame of mind, as it reminds me that life is not just about the acquisition of objects and wealth. It is actually fine for me to take myself off to my workshop from time to time to experience this simplicity. As Thoreau explains so eloquently, 'For more than five years I maintained myself thus solely by the labour of my own hands, and I found that, by working about six weeks in a year, I could meet all the expenses of living ... I am convinced, both by faith and experience, that to maintain oneself on this earth is not a hardship but a pastime, if we will live simply and wisely.'

I try to start calming my thoughts even before I have entered my place of work. I use my walk to the workshop as a kind of meditation – I feel the air as I step outside my back door, I listen to the wind through the tall pear tree in my garden and I connect to the world around me because doing this seems to reset my mind. Before I begin working, I always start with a tidy up. I sweep up any remnants of sawdust from the workshop floor, but it is not just about the place being clean – this act continues the process of quietening my thoughts. I carefully set out the tools I will use next to my workbench and I sharpen any necessary blades. The smell of the sawdust, the oils from my stone, the resin of the wood, have over the years become synonymous with this particular disposition, one of calm focus and awareness. It is the combination of technical knowledge and the sensitive connection to your discipline which makes good workmanship possible.

You will find these types of processes in many of the traditional crafts including, of course, the carpentry of Japan, a culture that is built on tradition. A hundred years ago, 85 per cent of Japan's population lived in wooden houses in the countryside. Wood is a plentiful resource in Japan whereas the stone in Japan is largely volcanic and difficult to build with. The people of Japan took up woodworking for practical purposes but they very quickly turned it into an art form and the traditional techniques and rituals that these master craftsmen learned are still in use to this day.

Rituals and respect are cornerstones of the Japanese craft philosophy, present in the way they use their tools, the way they understand the materials and the way they pass on their skills to the next generation. In Japanese carpentry, the apprentice would train for five years, through often menial tasks in which they learn the correct attitude and techniques. Woodwork is all about surfaces, edges and how they connect. An important part of the training is cleaning so that over this period they would see and be in contact with all kinds of surfaces and edges which is crucial to the making of a master craftsperson. It would take many years of maintaining the workshop and the tools before the apprentice was allowed to move on to woodworking. This respect for rituals and procedure is abundantly clear in the traditional Japanese carpenter's workshop, where there is no noise, there is unbelievable focus and there is a certain deference that is filled with the pride of belonging to the grand old tradition of carpentry that goes deep into Japan's past. Of course I am not suggesting that you should clean your workshop for five years before making this table, but the rituals and traditions of the workshop have survived for good reason. They have often developed over long periods of time and remain because they serve a useful purpose.

As well as the place and the ways in which we work, I also include the times we work as part of the rituals. When I was working on building sites there was a strict format of working 8:30am until 5pm, with lunchtime at 11am for an hour and a 20-minute break at 2pm. It is a different experience working alone, where there is no boss telling what you should or shouldn't be doing. The lack of rules sometimes encourages a late start, but if I do ease into the day, I will work into the evening. At other times I will get a bright and early start so I have the evening to relax, but either way I try to maintain some kind of structure because I know it will help me to be more productive.

Another important aspect of a structured day is that it encourages regular eating habits. Carpentry can be a highly physical job, but the concentration and focus needed for making accurate joints and measurements can also cause mental fatigue. Eating at regular intervals will keep your energy levels more consistent and will therefore make your work more consistent. I will have a large bowl of porridge and a head-clearing coffee in the morning. I prefer a substantial lunch with some form of slow-release carbohydrate and then I will try to have some fruit, nuts and a drink in the 2pm break. These breaks are physical breaks, but they should also be treated as mental breaks and I try to switch off from my work and just relax.

Of course, there are times when we don't want to be structured – when we want our imaginations to fly. Remember that the workshop structure and rituals are not our masters but they are there to help us. They should not control, but used correctly they are a means to get us into the right frame of mind and to sustain that frame of mind should we so wish.

The way I use rituals is so second nature to me now that I hardly notice they are rituals at all. When we spend time doing the things we want, the less we see them as an escape and the more they become just a part of life. I have to remind myself from time to time to follow the same procedures as I have always done because these procedures have transformed the amount of enjoyment I get from life. The workshop may be a sanctuary, but it is the rituals that create the peace. They induce a kind of utilitarian pleasure that is the companion to right thinking. They slow time to its natural pace, a pace that is reserved for only two experiences in life – happiness and contentment in our work. They stop us thinking about things that have happened in our lives or worrying about what will happen in the future. They help us to understand that all we ever really have is the given moment, and in this lies the power to be happy or not.

Dowels, biscuits, tongue and groove

It is time to take our prepared wood and joint the pieces together into a table top. The first stage is to arrange the boards in the order they will eventually be in as a finished table. There are two things to consider here – the aesthetics and the grain pattern. Aesthetically speaking, the board placement is a personal choice. The best way to go about finding the best order is to simply arrange and re-arrange until you are happy with what you see – a visually striking and organic pattern usually works well. Don't rush it, matching grain is an important part of working with solid wood and this is what you will be looking at forever once your table is complete.

Since my wood has such contrast between the classic light-cream healthy wood of the Ash and the dark discoloured wood that had been at the centre of my tree, I want to arrange the boards in such a way to accentuate these patterns. I want to avoid linear sections at the joints if I can so that the table top resembles the flow of forms I could see in the original slab of Ash. I eventually manage to get two beautiful strips of dark wood through the table top flanked on either side by the light wood. There was an especially nice light strip through the centre and one of the darker strips looked something like the top half of a giraffe.

Don't try to be too precise when it comes to the aesthetics. If, for example, you want only good, perfectly clear wood, free of any imperfections, the wood wasted to get this perfection would be too great. Besides, the knots, grain and discolouration add character and make a piece unique and interesting. When it comes to the grain, the ideal arrangement should be to alternate the end-grain pattern. This means that as you look at the end grain of the boards, the half circular patterns of each board should face in different directions, in effect making something like a sine wave of grain lines. This arrangement will result in the boards being more resistant to cupping. Cupping is mostly caused by shrinking of the wood because as the wood dries it wants to become concave on the topside. It is often worse in plane-sawn wood than in quarter-sawn because the radial shrinkage is exaggerated. A simple way to visualise how this will affect the wood is to picture the arc of the growth rings trying to flatten themselves out. Since my wood has been dried and is by all accounts stable, I hope this will be less of an issue.

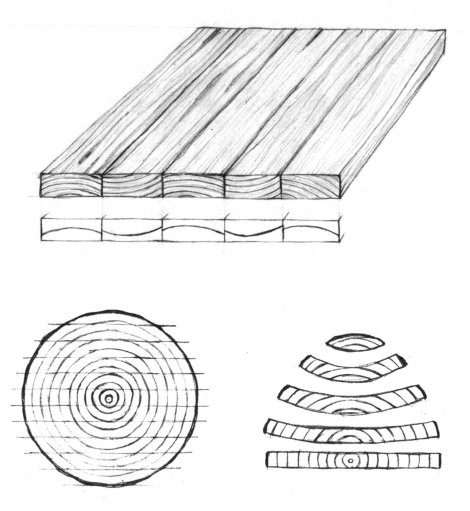

There is often a compromise between the ideal aesthetic arrangement and the ideal structural arrangement. I would usually say that all structural decisions should overrule any aesthetic decisions, but in this case there are many variables and it is more sensible to use a certain amount of your own judgement on the matter. If the ideal end-grain pattern unduly affects the colour and clarity of the table-top aesthetics, it may not be necessary to change the order of your boards depending on how extreme the end-grain lines interact with each other. In my case the ideal aesthetic arrangement did impact on the ideal grain pattern, but by simply swapping one of the darker boards around the issue was quickly resolved. I suspect my tree had grown on an angle so the paths of the grain are not especially consistent and these inconsistent grain patterns ultimately help me get the look I want.

I have my final arrangement, I mark the table top with location lines so we can return the boards to the same position and it is now time to begin the process of jointing the wood. There are several methods for joining a table top, which include dowelling, biscuit jointing, making tongue and groove or simply end-to-end gluing. Because of the tools we have available, we decide to make a kind of tongue and groove, but since you may not have all the same tools available I will explain the other methods also.

Dowel joints

The advantages of the dowel method are that it can be performed relatively quickly and that it is possible with hand tools alone. Dowels are basically cylindrical-shaped pieces of wood that, once glued, act in the same way as a simple mortise and tenon joint. Commercially made dowels have flutes to relieve air pressure as they are inserted, which also ensure they are not glue starved. The trick with any connecting method is to be accurate when marking out and this is certainly the case with dowelling. Use a marking gauge to indicate the centre of the edge of the boards. Next, you will need to mark the positions of the dowels by drawing vertical lines on the edge of the boards. The more dowels you use, the more gluing area you have and the more strength the joint will have.

Select a drill bit that matches the size of dowel you will use and drill holes at each of the marked positions. It is important that you drill vertically so the dowels can be inserted straight. Next you will need to drill corresponding holes in the joining piece of wood either by using the same method or by inserting small spikes called centre points which will make an imprint where you need to drill the holes. Drill the holes in the joining board at the same depth as the first board. Finally, glue the dowels and the end grain on both pieces of wood and fit the joint together.

Biscuit joints

Biscuit joints are also a quick and easy method of effectively joining boards especially with the addition of the specific power tool designed for the job, aptly called the biscuit jointer. The biscuits are commercially bought elliptical discs which fit into matching slots in the two pieces of wood joining them together and again acting like simple mortise and tenon joints. Biscuit jointing is a very similar procedure to dowelling, but has an advantage over the dowel because it has long grain which forms a stronger joint.

First place the two edges of wood to be joined together side by side and draw a square line on both with your combination square to mark where the centre of each slot will be. Set the height of the biscuit jointer blade to cut a slot in the middle of each piece of wood. Adjust the blade to the correct size of biscuit, align the machine with the pencil marks on the edge of the wood and machine the elliptical slot. Insert the biscuits into each slot and if the joints fit, apply glue and join the two pieces together.

End-to-end gluing

The primary concern when end-to-end gluing is to ensure the edges that will be joined are perfectly square and true; this is especially important since there are no dowels or biscuits to help. Periodically check for gaps which will show you an area that needs to be planed. When you are happy the two boards fit perfectly together, simply glue and clamp the boards together until the glue has set.

Tongue and groove joints

Our preferred method of joining the boards is to make a kind of tongue and groove joint. We don't have dowels or a biscuit jointer, but the fact that we have a table saw means that making tongue and groove joints is a relatively easy procedure. The first step is to make the tongues and for this we simply rip up (cut parallel to the grain) some 6mm plywood into strips of around 200mm x 26mm. Once the 26mm tongue is split between two pieces of wood, it will result in a 13mm tongue fitting snuggly within two 15mm grooves. We block plane and sand the edges to make it easier to insert them into the grooves we will make.

Next we cut grooves with the table saw through the edges of the wood that will be joined. The table saw has a standard blade so it takes a few passes to make the groove wide enough to fit the 6mm ply tongues. We keep the boards laid out in the position of the table top to avoid

getting confused about the order. When handling wood at this stage it is important to take care and not bash the edges which can spoil the board joints. The groove is cut centrally along the length of the board edges, stopping just before the ends. The face edge symbol marked in pencil is still in use, ensuring each pass through the table saw is consistent and also helping us to avoid cutting or grooving the wrong piece of wood.

With all the grooves complete, it is time to check the position of the tongue and grooves with a dry run. This is essential; there is nothing worse than the messy fumbling of glue-coated carpenter's fingers trying to desperately release a joint that won't fully close before it dries. Past failures have forever instilled in me the value of the dry run, especially working on hot days when glue dries too fast and attempts to release joints by pouring boiling water over them have ended badly.

The joints look really good, with only minute discrepancies, but we still briefly clamp up the wood to make sure that even these fractions of millimetres could be pulled together and there were no obstructions such as a tongue being too wide for a groove. All is well in the world of table making; it is time for some eggs from Jean and Ernest's chickens next door and then for the afternoon, we had planned a visit to a local tree surgeon for his perspective on my tree wood.

Fraxinus excelsior: getting to know my tree

'The good life is one inspired by love and guided by knowledge.'

BERTRAND RUSSELL

The skills of the carpenter are learned skills, skills that are improved with experience, with mastering the hand positions over time and gradually developing a touch and a sensitivity to the material. But there are always things that lie beneath the surface. Taking a closer look at the science and the history behind what is visible gives us a wider perspective. The acquisition of this information makes the whole process more interesting, given the more we know about anything in life, the more invested we are and usually the more we care.

I like the feeling of opening the door on a new subject, of awakening the detective. We all have this within us, an instinctive desire to look around the next corner. And each time we look around the corner, a new set of mysteries shows itself to us. For every answer, there are a multitude of questions and the more we find out, the more we realise we don't know. But understanding the various mechanisms behind a new subject takes reading. When embarking on a new project, I like to acquire as much information about the subject as I can, then I try to let all this information settle for a while, letting it slowly absorb like the nutrients of fallen leaves into the soil. I find in this way my subconscious will gradually put things in order and it will pick out the relevant information as and when I need it. This information or knowledge will eventually help to grow new ideas or inspire new thoughts.

In this case, I want to know more about my Ash tree – what makes Ash the way it is, what has been our relationship to Ash over the years? I want to become closer to my tree, to understand it so I can treat it the way it wants to be treated. I begin by reading all I can find on the Common Ash, but I also think an important part of all research is to talk to people who have a close connection to the subject matter. My cousin Robbie took me to a local tree surgeon and friend, Ken from Emery Landscaping, and I pieced together my knowledge from a mixture of Ken's perspective and my own research.

Fraxinus excelsior, or the Common Ash, is part of the genus *Fraxinus* and contains about 70 species that are native to Central and North America, Europe and Asia. There are three species of Ash in Europe but by far the most common is the suitably named Common Ash. Its growing area ranges as far north as Norway and as south as the Pyrenees, from the west coast of Ireland right through to Russia. Ash is the third most common broad-leaved tree in Britain after the Oak and the Birch. It usually grows to heights of between 20m and 40m, it has a beautiful grey-green bark which is smooth when young and cracks with age. Often you will find it covered in moss and lichen. The leaves are easily identified, pairs of leaflets on a central stalk, with dark leaves on top and a lighter shade underneath.

In Scandinavian mythology the huge Ash known as Yggdrasil was the tree of life, the branches of which extend far into the heavens. In many cultures, it is regarded as a healing tree. In Britain up until the 18th century it was used as a treatment for weak limbs – a child was passed through a young Ash tree naked, in a relic of pre-Christian magic. It has more superstitions associated with it than any other British tree, from anti-rheumatic treatments to wart curing to good luck charms protecting sailors at sea. Children would wish an Ash tree 'good day' and phrases such as 'never harm an Ash tree' and 'respect the Ash tree' hark back to these mystical roots.

I asked Ken what he considered to be the main characteristics of the Ash tree and his first thoughts were about the wood itself rather than the superstitions which was encouraging.

'The wood of the Ash tree is a very strong wood. It has long fibres and a good tensile strength. It is classed as an indigenous tree and you will often see Ash stands around here in big rings. Where they've been coppiced, the root stocks have been there for a thousand years but it will keep sending up healthy shoots – this new growth is good for logs and poles and shafts. All trees have their natural coppice period; for the Ash tree it is usually 11 or 12 years. The wood will mature on an Ash tree after about 20 years. This is faster than lots of other species of tree. This mature wood is stronger and has a greater tensile strength.'

Ash doesn't like waterlogged ground, but providing the soil is right, it will tolerate a wide range of conditions. On a good site, Ash is fast growing and it is more prolific than Oak. Ash trees can typically live for 200 years, but they can survive much longer and a coppiced Ash will produce good straight shoots indefinitely. It grows fast for the first 40–60 years, but traditionally it was felled before this because the wood was so useful. Ash yields more than any other British hardwood tree other than Beech. Its resilience and speed

of growth made Ash an invaluable tree on small farms and cottages. It is still the commonest tree in coppice woodland across Britain and it is probably the most versatile raw material in the countryside. I ask Ken if he has any Ash and he immediately points at various locations across his land.

'The Ash tree is very successful, it has a very nice fecundity. They can put out a lot of seeds and they establish very rapidly; they will grow quicker than anything really apart from maybe Sycamore. Part of its strength lies underground. They have a huge root system which goes down very deep and because of this, you will quite often see them growing in harsh conditions like on these scree slopes. Nothing else will grow, but Ash will. This extensive root system is part of how they survive really.'

The Ash tree puts out a vast quantity of winged seeds known as 'keys' and the wind will scatter them over wide and substantial distances. They produce millions of these seeds, which make Ash a prolific natural propagator. This has helped to make it one of the largest contributors to broad-leaved forest regeneration in Britain. This prolific nature and the speed at which it can colonise new ground may also have contributed it to being seen as somewhat of a weed tree by some over the years. Even today it is still often (but unfairly in my mind) regarded as a second-class tree, behind the Beech and the Oak.

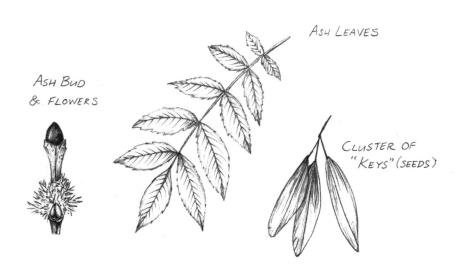

Ash Leaves

Ash Bud & Flowers

Cluster of "Keys" (seeds)

A more sensible outlook towards the Ash would be to value its productivity and marvel at its natural hardiness and ability to survive and grow. Ash trees rarely live as long or develop such character as the Oak or Beech and therefore do not often have the same status as a landmark or a boundary tree. The Ash tree may not have the same majestic structure as some trees and it may not have enjoyed the widespread acclaim, but its humble standing is perhaps befitting of this practical workhorse of the countryside. Ken shares some more of his knowledge:

'I know the Ash for its use in a wheel, as far as I know, again because of its tensile strength and its ability to withstand shock. And they used to make bows out of Ash. They famously used Yew, because Yew has its natural lamination and the bow would last longer. But I believe Ash made the best bows, they just didn't have the longevity. They would try to pick one with a natural curve to make it easier to shape and to reduce the stresses on it.'

The prolific nature of Ash has ensured it has been a cheap and sustainable resource making it a real hero of the functioning British countryside. But to attribute this to its prevalence alone would be to do the tree a great disservice. It is the Ash wood itself which has secured its place in British history.

Ash wood has the magical combination of being strong, light and elastic. Ash glues well, it is easily bent, it cleaves willingly, and is readily polished, stained and varnished. It is a supremely versatile wood, from lobster pots to ladders, walking sticks to wheel hubs, its adaptability seemingly knows no bounds.

Ash has been used for working the land and for farming purposes for millennia. Ploughs, wheelbarrows, blocks for pulleys, fishing rods, bean poles, handles for spades, shovels, forks and scythes have all been fashioned from this tree. Its suitability for handles also extends to striking tools. Hammers, axes and chisels have all benefited from the properties of Ash wood. Ash is perfect for handles generally because of its resistance to sudden impact. It is also very consistent and it is said the more you use an Ash handle, the better it gets.

Ash has a similar suitability for sports equipment for much the same reasons – the wood's combination of strength and elasticity. The elasticity of wood generally speaking is its ability to return to its original state; the opposite of elasticity is brittleness. Ash has all the attributes for sporting equipment – it is not too heavy, it doesn't splinter, no other wood is better at withstanding sudden shocks. An important part of making these sporting goods is Ash's ability to be successfully bent and this attribute also lends itself to the making of other equipment. Ash is considered to be one of the very best woods for bending because it stays in its bent shape forever, whereas other hardwoods can try to revert back their original form. Bending Ash for sleds and skis has been done since Neolithic times. Ash sledges were used by the Norwegian explorer Roald Amundsen who famously beat Robert Falcon Scott to reach the South Pole. Polar sledges are still often made from Ash to this day.

This ability to bend and retain its strength meant Ash was one of the three different woods used in the manufacture of wheels. Ash is used to make the felloes or the rims of the wheel, while the hubs or knaves were always Elm and the spokes were made from Oak. Ash was prolific in the manufacture of various forms of weaponry. Ash made lances, bows, axes, spears (Achilles' spear was made of Ash in Homer's The Iliad). The best wooden arrows are still made from Ash today because Ash can withstand the forces involved while retaining the stiffness needed to fly a straight arrow. It was also well known to children that Ash would make the best catapult from a natural fork – again elasticity playing its role.

ASH FELLOE

OAK SPOKE

ELM HUB

Ash is also an important wood in the production of walking sticks. The wood has the necessary springiness able to take the constant collisions with the ground while maintaining the strength to support a person's weight. The Ash for a walking stick would usually be taken from two- or three-year-old growth. To form the handle, the wood would be heated in damp sand and bent in a curved vice. It is also possible to make a natural curve by planting at an angle in the ground so the growth of the tree rises almost at right angles. I ask Ken what he uses his Ash trees for and the answer conveys a similar message to many people in the countryside, reinforcing Ash's reputation for being good firewood.

'I find the best wood for burning is Beech, it leaves very little waste, but Ash is also excellent firewood. But all well-seasoned wood burns and the best fires burn on a mixture of woods. They say you can burn Ash wood green, but you should dry it. It will still have moisture in it which will be smoky and it won't be good for your burner. It can leave deposits of tar in the chimney which can cause fires.'

Ash is a dense wood and it contains a lot of cellulose which means it burns nice and slowly. Ash also splits easily – the main reason for this is the grain is often in a good straight line parallel to the direction in which the tree grows. This has probably contributed to its reputation as great firewood. Chopped wood speeds up the rate at which the wood dries by increasing the volume to surface area of each log. The long fibres are unusual in their ability to split when both green and dry. The top heat-producing woods in Britain are Birch, Ash, Oak and Beech, with Beech at the top, although there does seem to be some debate about this.

Ken is keen to discuss the ecological aspects of the wood and like most people, he understands Oak as the most important species, but ecosystems are complicated things and research shows that Ash forms its own important functions within a forest.

'The Ash doesn't have the ecological carrying capacity of something like an Oak tree, but it does have its own individual ecological functions. Ash as standing timber will support more wildlife – you will get stag beetle, for example, in piles of rotting Ash. The larvae can be five years of burrowing away before they come out, but they do like Ash because it's a good wood. Ash is also good as part of a forest because they let light through, which means you get lots of particular species of plants growing.'

There is currently a concern in Britain with the *Hymenoscyphus* (formerly *Chalara*) *fraxineus*, more commonly known as Ash dieback, which threatens the British Ash population. Ash dieback was first observed in the

Baltic States of Latvia and Lithuania. Across continental Europe, 70 per cent of trees have been infected with disastrous effect. Besides the loss of the Ash, it will have an impact on many Ash-associated species from mammals and birds to invertebrates, fungi and lichens. Other trees can fill the gaps left in the canopy by the Ash, but no single tree species is able to provide a suitable alternative for all Ash-associated species. Interestingly Ash trees have been a good replacement for Elm trees after their widespread loss due to Dutch Elm disease. They have been especially important for epiphytes (plants that grow on other plants) because both trees have a high bark pH and both support similar species. There is some evidence from continental Europe that older, mature Ash trees can survive infection and continue to provide their landscape and wildlife benefits for some time. However, the best hope for the long-term future is to identify the genetic factors which enable some Ash trees to tolerate or resist infection, and using these to breed new generations of tolerant Ash trees.

I wanted to know if there was anything that Ken's experienced eyes could tell me about my Ash, and I showed him photos on my camera of the Ash slabs.

'It's a nice thick piece of Ash. Ash doesn't tend to twist much in general, so it should be okay. There is some nice straight grain here. I'm guessing you will use this for the legs, but you will know more about this than me. You can see there's been a branch here, but where the branch has fallen off it looks as if there has been some infection in there, that's what the dark stain is. The wound has eventually calloused over and it's been occluded. The tree reacts when it has been wounded. There are margins between the annual rings and the tree will set up chemical barriers. These barriers are resistant to most fungi. You can see where the tree has actually managed to contain what has affected it and the wood that has formed after that has been protected. You can see the scar on that Ash over there.'

Ken shows us an Ash tree close by that grows on the boundary of the field opposite. He points out a gnarly lump of wood, about football size, that protrudes from the trunk about five metres in the air, the same height as it begins to split off into branches.

'When they get over 40 or 50 years old, there's a particular fungus which affects them called *Inonotus hispidus*. The wood can appear sound in the early stages, but as time goes on it can weaken the timber. It takes all the tensile strength out of the wood and it becomes vulnerable to sudden impact. It can cause branches to break or fall in stormy weather. It's quite well known to beware when building a tree house in Ash. Sometimes the fungus will penetrate further. It will gradually become a sunken legion on the stem and it will be rotting in the middle. It will feed on the heartwood which is essentially dead; the sapwood has more resistance to infection. When we are trimming a tree, we have to cut branches off in a particular way to avoid this. Where the branch wood peters out, that's where it originates from so if we're pruning, we wouldn't cut into the main wood itself. Then the tree will just cut it off, the sap flow will stop and the vessels get closed off. In saying this, your wood will still be solid and strong. You quite often get patterns like this in Ash trees.'

This may have been the reason the tree became structurally unsafe. It would be impossible to know now, but for me the infection and the discolouration was part of the tree's story and it would help me to remember that my wood was once a tree and that it had lived a long life before it was my table. Ash may not have the same place in our hearts as something like the Oak, but I wonder if even on a practical front the Ash is still a rather undervalued tree. Either way, with the knowledge I now have I would never look on any Ash tree in quite the same light again.

Sash clamps and glue

It is a new morning in Darley Dale and as I drink an early coffee and wait for my cousin to return from the school run, I watch the early morning birds replenish their tiny bodies with the vital sustenance that will allow winter survival. It is a pleasant sight to my city eyes seeing the usual urban feeders such as robins, blue tits and great tits, fraternising with the more rural species of black caps, siskin and a lesser spotted woodpecker. In the near distance, I watch a treecreeper work its way up the trunks of pine trees searching for food in front of the kitchen window, before fluttering down to their bases to repeat the procedure again.

On Robbie's return, we open up the doors and eagerly turn on the lights to view the table top once again. The patterns in the wood I had imagined from the evening before didn't disappoint. Today's jobs of gluing and clamping the table top permanently together should once again be relatively straightforward because of the good progress we made the day before.

First we check all is good with the table top. There seems to be some slight movement with one of the boards – a small gap had opened up, but it was insignificant enough. It probably happened because we had cut the width of the boards, potentially releasing tension in the wood. The tighter the joint, the better it is going to be, but in this type of scenario it is wise to remember that wood is not always a predictable material. It can be tempting to keep on trimming a piece of wood in an attempt to make it straight but the subsequent release of tension in the wood bends it further. Sometimes you have to use your judgement and make the call to just use the piece of wood in its current condition because it is probably as good as it is going to get. In our case it was in the middle of the table top and once clamped together and glued up, the other boards would help to keep it straight.

We dismantle the table top and stack it in order on another surface before laying out the sash clamps on the gluing table (these are sometimes referred to as sash cramps). We set the clamps to a width just wider than the table top would be by adjusting the pins. This is important because once the boards are laid on top and glued together it will be difficult to lift the sash clamps in order to adjust them. Also be sure to leave enough room for two thin pieces of wood which will protect your table top when the clamps are tightened.

Next it is time for gluing up. You should have a variety of glues in your workshop because different glues have different properties and will therefore be more suited to a range of jobs. The most common types of glue to have in any workshop are PVA (polyvinyl acetate) for solid wood and some form of resin glue usually for veneer work, but PVA is good for this job. We stand

the boards to be glued up on their side edges. We glue the tongues and insert them and then liberally apply glue to the edge surfaces. Sometimes you can apply the glue directly from the bottle, but in our case a brush helps so we can be sure there is glue on the more difficult to reach places next to the tongues. Once glued, we push the boards together and check their position by using the location lines we had drawn on the board faces.

We repeat this process with all the remaining boards and when our table top gluing is complete, we carefully clean all the surfaces with a clean cloth and clean water. I will often clean wood with a natural cotton or linen rag so I can be sure there will be no colour penetrating the wood which at this stage in proceedings is non-protected bare wood and prone to staining. Most glues are water based and evaporation is a part of the drying process. You should try not to glue up in temperatures below 15 degrees Celsius. In our winter workshop we are below this so indulge ourselves with the use of a heater to warm up proceedings, but since the wood could be left clamped up in the same position for a while we are not unduly concerned. Under normal conditions, PVA glue can be dry within hours, but it is worth mentioning that if you are working in a very humid area you may also need to leave your clamps in position for a longer time, even if it is above 15 degrees Celsius. Once glued joints have dried, they quite often become the strongest part of the table and if you were to one day try to smash up your beautiful table, it may indeed be the glued joints which remain intact the longest.

The final stage is to clamp the table top together while the glue dries. Before tightening, we place a thin offcut from our Ash boards along the edges of the table top in order to protect it from the tightening jaws of the sash clamps. The bars of the sash clamps should be placed alternately top and bottom at a distance of around 30cm. Once they are all in position it is important to tighten them slowly in stages, by applying consistent pressure gradually to each of the clamps. If, for example, you tighten all the bottom clamps first, there is no support on top and the large amounts of pressure involved could easily buckle and the boards could burst out of the rack with potentially disastrous consequences. The bars of the clamps should be placed close to the table top for stability. If you are using some woods (especially Oak with iron clamps), it is a good idea to protect the wood from oxidisation marks by either wrapping the clamps with masking tape or placing a protective cloth or waxed paper beneath the clamps so they do not come into contact with your table-top surface.

We tighten the clamps hard, slowly drawing together the tiny gaps until they are imperceptible. The table top looks great, the grains match well – so well in fact, it isn't obvious where the joins are. The boards are actually reasonably flat – I suppose I had expected there to be more inconsistencies. At this stage, if your boards are not flat it is possible to use G-clamps on the joins, again with some protective wood in place until the glue dries.

Once dry, the table top would be cut to the exact dimensions and it would be ready for planing and sanding. We have our usual straighten up and as I clear the workshop of excess scraps of wood, I happen across one of the long thin strips of Ash we had cut from the boards. It is so thin I thought I would just snap it in two instead of cutting it on the chop saw. As I tried, the strip bent so effortlessly it was immediately apparent that I could never snap this wood with my hands or indeed with any part of my body. With all I had recently learned about Ash wood, I now knew this was because of the long Ash fibres and the high elasticity of the wood, but previously I had only understood this in theory. In reality the effects were actually quite extraordinary – the wood bent into a tight circle with ease and it became obvious why Ash was, for example, the wheel maker's rim material of choice and why it had enjoyed such a versatile and useful history within the British rural countryside.

Awakening ancestors

'Because an experience is itself within the whole of life, the whole of life is present in it too.'

HANS-GEORG GADAMER

Our work was done for now and it was time for me to go back to London. I had not found working in a cold and rather bleak January especially easy at times. This, I fear, is the result of the privileges of modern comforts, of central heating, electric kettles and flexible work schedules. My cousin Robbie returned to the house to make a cup of tea and I sat on a wooden stool in the doorway of Darley Dale workshop looking out across the fields of withered and faded grasses swaying slightly in a calm winter breeze. The sun had disappeared now over the barn to the west, the moon was already on the night watch hanging over the tree tops in a dusky green-blue sky. There is a feeling I get sometimes when I look towards the moon, a moon that has always been there, unmoved by the endeavours of the living world. I feel as though my eyes are not my own and it is easy to imagine another's vision from a time gone by. On this evening the feeling was stronger. The day had been one of hand tools and glue, of hot drinks and hard work; it felt as though I could peek through a crack in time and glimpse something of a working day of old.

The more you learn about carpentry, the more the connection with your tools and with the wood extends past the present moment. When I see an old piece of furniture, I love to see the marks of a maker, a pencil mark underneath a table top, a slightly misshapen dovetail, a tiny nick of the block plane. I am taken back to the time when it was built, I imagine the hand that crafted it, and for a brief moment, the spirit of the maker is perceived like the footprints of an invisible ghost.

When you spend time making a table, a part of you enters the soul of that table, but just as important is that the table becomes a part of you. By this I mean the act of working on a table brings us into contact not just with our tools and the wood, but with our past. In my life as a carpenter I am definitely not a purist – I love my power tools and they can make life easier and often make work better, but when we use traditional tools and techniques to make an object, we are connecting to the skills of our ancestors and with this we are gaining an understanding of who we are.

The philosopher Hans-Georg Gadamer (*below*) said, 'history does not belong to us but we belong to it.' He believed that when viewing historical objects, we should not view time as a gulf to be bridged. 'Its distance is filled with the continuity of tradition, which sheds light on our understanding.' Gadamer viewed the process of understanding our lives and ourselves as having a conversation with history; it is through this dialogue or what he called 'the fusion of horizons' that our understanding of life reaches a deeper, richer level.

For me, this perspective on how we perceive the past is especially appropriate when we consider carpentry. The ability to construct things from wood goes right back to the Neolithic period and the use of wood for toolmaking and for building shelters was significant in determining our conversion from nomadic hunters and herdsmen into settled farmers. Wooden objects played an invaluable role in the development of early settlements, from farming tools, to boats and to basic furniture such as the table. The feeling of being linked to thousands of years of ancestors is one that I find humbling and inspiring and I often feel that when working with wood, I am showing respect to past generations and in my own way I am helping to celebrate our craft traditions and our creative history.

Being connected to the past through the work that we do at times feels like a little story that continues from generation to generation of craftsmen and women. William Morris, the recognised leader of the Arts and Crafts movement, puts it well in his writings from Useful Work versus Useless Toil: 'A man at work, making something which he feels will exist because he is working at it and wills it, is exercising the energies of his mind and soul as well as his body. Memory and imagination help as he works. Not only his own thoughts, but the thoughts of the men of past ages guide his hands; and, as part of the human race, he creates.'

It makes me wonder at the limits of this perspective, how far back in time we can associate with past ages. The carpenters that made refectory tables for monks, the trestle table makers of the Roman Empire or even the early platform constructors of ancient Egypt. Who can really ever know what the thoughts of these crafters were, but to spend a day working in a similar manner gives us as good an insight as any (*below*: a traditional carpentry worskhop).

I wonder whether in the future there could be a time when carpentry is seen as an ancient tradition. Some might argue that time is already here, but to me carpentry is a timeless pursuit. If a computer programmer were to take their knowledge with them to a future time, I would expect the functionality of that knowledge to be limited or largely useless. But if you imagine for a moment a Japanese master craftsman from the 16th century being transported into our world, the skills would translate immediately and may even surpass our current expertise. In 1,000 years from now or in 10,000 years from now, regardless of the technology that is available, the tools I have used will still do the same job and the hands that plane the table surface will still move in the same manner as they do today.

A part of me feels anxious for future generations as I wonder if the simple pleasures of making that are such an important part of being human will gradually fade. In some ways, it makes me feel lucky to be alive at this time, to have a view of the future and strong links to the past, but I suppose every generation feels a need to preserve or rekindle the things which are being replaced. To my mind there will always be people interested in making themselves a table for the very same reasons I want to. A need to challenge themselves and bring something into the world that is not just bought, a desire to light a fire underneath the stress-free, non-eventful lives we seem so keen to create – a progression that adds comfort but also seems to strip away our sense of purpose. The things that I seek, the feeling of wanting to be connected to the world around me, of wanting my work to have a meaning, they are addressed through craftwork. For this reason the makers will always remain because this is what the living do – they keep the things that are useful to them, like the hammer or the handshake or love.

I may have found it hard in the cold, but the rewards for this type of work are felt on an invisible dimension. The sense of well-being that accompanies physical hard work is difficult to recreate without it. There may not have been central heating, there wasn't even a clock in this workshop, but the time felt like our own and our decisions were defined solely by our fatigue and the fading light of day. The dropping temperature directed my move indoors and the vision of the moon that had awakened the ancestors within me now turned them back into ghosts. In a hundred years from now each of us that is alive today will be ancestors of the past and as I lock the workshop door and glance at the table top, I wonder if my table will one day allow my ghost to emerge in somebody else's moment of passing contemplation.

Part 3
The Table
Base

Trestles: legs, aprons, rails and stretchers

It is a cold morning in early March, the spring has been postponed and through the night Darley Dale was the recipient of a late dumping of snow. Although it was only a few inches, snowdrifts have accumulated over the weeks, their twisted wind-carved forms rising out of the ground, resisting the thaw. The temperature has dragged itself upwards to a measly 4 degrees, but the best course of action in these conditions is to cast the cold from your mind, put another layer on and get down to some physical work. Today's job is to make the two trestles that will support the table top and prepare the aprons and the central stretcher for base assembly. Much of the morning has involved using the surfacer and thicknesser to prepare the wood for the legs, aprons, rails and the stretcher in the same way as we had prepared the wood for the table top by feeding it through the machines until the wood was consistently straight on all sides. Similarly to the table top, most of the wood had held up well in the drying process. Just one piece had bent dramatically, but again we had accounted for this by having extra wood for this eventuality. Seeing the way this piece had bent so much brought it home just how important it is to choose the right piece of wood for particular component parts. We had carefully picked the straightest grained wood for the legs and these had kept their shape well. If we had not taken care with this choice and the legs had bent completely out of shape, it would have meant buying more wood.

The original dimensions of the table had changed. I had always intended to get the most out of the tree slab and maximise the table size.

In my first designs I had decided the minimum size for my table should be 178cm x 91cm in order to sit four people comfortably or six people if necessary. The new dimensions of the table top are now 175cm x 94cm which is close enough to suit its purpose. These changes in dimensions mean adjusting the sizes for my trestles slightly on the widths, the heights would remain the same, finishing to 76cm. We set the table legs back 4cm from the edges of the table and the new trestle width is now 86cm. Scenarios such as these are not uncommon in carpentry; circumstances can change, wood can be damaged, sizes are altered. You have to be able to adjust at times, to be flexible, which is why leaving your wood 'as long as you can for as long as you can' is so useful as it gives you more options should something unexpected arise. Adjusting sizes does increase the possibility of making mistakes, so I find it best to get my carpenter's sketchbook out again and re-do my cut lists and re-draw the alterations properly, including the sizes of the joints so there is no confusion. It is useful to draw an actual size template of the trestle onto a piece of plywood and work to these

measurements. This has several advantages: it will help you to make both your trestles the same size and if the dimensions of the table turn out to be a success, then you can easily recreate the trestles by using the stencil to replicate. You will often find different-shaped stencils hanging up in joinery workshops for this purpose.

Once the legs, aprons and rails had been cut to their new length, a groove is cut into the aprons at 10mm deep and 12mm from the top edge of the apron. We use a table saw for this because we have one available. You could also use a router or you could potentially even chisel out the grooves in sections. This groove will eventually be used to fix the table top to the table base with buttons or fasteners. We run a block plane over the sharp edges and then sand down the legs, aprons and rails with an 80-grade sandpaper and a sanding block (they are sanded at this stage because it would be more difficult once the table is assembled).

We now have all the component parts ready for the next stage. It is approaching lunch, so we decide to have a break and ready ourselves for the making of the mortise and tenon joints. There is no sense in rushing. It is better to check our measurements, to lay out all the necessary tools, to sharpen the chisels. Miscalculations at this point would be critical, given that we had accounted for misdemeanours in the drying process, but we hadn't accounted for mistakes in the cutting process. We do not want to buy more wood because of an error, not just because it might look and act differently over time, but also because it would have been a shame to make the table out of two different trees.

Before lunchtime, we participate in some farming essentials – a novelty and a pleasure for a city dweller such as I. We collect the haylage (silage made from grass which has been partially dried) from a neighbouring local farm up the road using Robbie's tractor with a menacing spike attachment on the front arm, before feeding the horses and sheep. A flock of redwings gathered on a nearby Hawthorn, refuelling themselves for a trip to their northern breeding territories, but they disappear across the field as we approach to feed the animals. Then it's back to the house to fuel ourselves so our capacity for concentration is at its maximum for the afternoon's work.

Right thinking

'The mind is everything. What you think, you become.'

SIDDHĀRTHA GAUTAMA

There is a certain condition I have grown to recognise in life which I refer to as 'right thinking'. It is not easy to define because it is not one thing, but a mixture of thoughts and feelings and attitudes. I would describe it as a combination of calm focus and a disciplined determination, the result of which is a better quality of carpentry. There are rules I like to give myself when working which are all really just different manifestations of this right thinking attitude. The first and most basic principle is to do a job properly. This is a simple concept but it is not always as easy to accomplish as it sounds. I have learned from experience that rushing into a job (for example the mortise and tenons) seldom pays off. By far the most efficient way to work in carpentry is to take the time to do things in the right way, in the right order. Sometimes you have to be hard on yourself if you want to achieve a high standard of work. By this, I do not mean pushing yourself physically or forcing a certain mental attitude, it is more the non-acceptance of poor craftsmanship or mediocre work.

Part of this respect towards your work is being able to recognise if your head is not in the right place. If you are tense or anxious then this will always show up in what you do. I know some people who like to use work to help them feel better about their problems in life and I can understand this, but my advice is to use the rituals I have talked about to get your mind in a better place before you get your chisel out and put it to the wood. If the rituals still haven't calmed you, sometimes you have to be prepared to walk away from your work and return when your thoughts have settled. To do a job properly means knowing the right pace. In commercial carpentry the speed with which you can accomplish a particular job is more often than not associated with a good 'chippie'. But quality will always be more important than speed – a carpenter who does good work at their own pace will be thought of as slow, but the carpenter who works fast and whose work is unsatisfactory will be thought of simply as bad. Making a table for yourself doesn't follow these rules. Since the work is your own, you should take the time to do things in the right way, which will also help you to enjoy the experience more. Sharpen your pencil, accurately mark your cut lines, take care making the cuts and chiselling out the wood. It takes a little learning, this slower pace, especially if you have been conditioned to working in the commercial world. You are inviting time to be a part of the whole process – the feeling should be as if you are travelling at a consistent, pleasant pace and not trying to go faster or slower than the world intended you to.

Another rule I have is to finish each stage. The best way to work whether running a business or as an amateur carpenter at home is to split the table-making process into a series of digestible elements. At the end of each stage it is useful to stand back and look at the work – you should be satisfied it is accurate and complete before you decide to move on. This also avoids what I call the 'kick-on effect' whereby a simple problem will be magnified over a series of stages like a kind of bodge resonance. Say, for example, you have a blunt pencil and you think you'll just go ahead and mark your tenon, so the joint you end up making is out and it kicks out the apron, and then the table base is no longer square and so you adjust your table top and so on. It can be really tempting, especially with some of the more technical elements to skip a job and get some of the simpler tasks done first, but I advise against this. You will have to face it eventually and changing back and forth from jobs means changing tools, which can mean re-sharpening blades or if your workshop is small, it can mean putting tools away as well getting new ones out. All of this spoils the flow of your work, it eats into your day, but more importantly it disrupts the mind and it can take time to get back into the right headspace for good working again. The order of the various processes and the ways in which they are accomplished are often part of a tradition – these traditions exist for a reason. They have developed over hundreds of years, with carpenters gradually ironing out problems and adjusting to mistakes so that you don't have to.

I also find it useful to connect each of the various stages of the process. Understanding and being conscious of how things fit together will help you to reduce mistakes, at least any significant errors. It is possible to be too involved and sometimes we just get so close to a particular job that we forget how it fits into the whole design. The most obvious of these is the mortise and tenon joints, but even with basic things like dimensions it is good to remain aware of the whole table. Remember that right thinking also includes how you feel about the making process. For some this comes naturally, for others it is more difficult to grasp. Throughout this book, knowledge about traditions, the structure of wood and the living tree are trickled through the narrative in the hope it will connect you to the project so you enjoy it more. Right thinking can be learned, but it can also be accessed through the very natural process of simply caring about what you do. And finally, the part that I still find difficult – you should learn to reward yourself. To be over critical can be of detriment to your work. You should remember this is what separates table making from the meaningless office jobs – the responsibility is all yours, so if you do a job well and you are satisfied, you should allow yourself to be pleased. This will also help you believe you can achieve the same results in the stages that follow.

The concept of right thinking goes all the way back to ancient times and the use of rules or guidelines to teach a particular quality of life runs the course of human history. Sometimes they hang on a particular religion or political movement, sometimes they are part of a set of beliefs. The example I gain greatest enjoyment from and the one that feels most appropriate when translating it to carpentry is that of Siddh rtha Gautama, later known as Buddha, 'the enlightened one'. Buddhism is understood as a religion by some, but I prefer to think of it as a philosophy. Gautama did not act as a medium between God and man, rather his search for truth followed a path of philosophical reasoning, a journey which he maintained was available to all. The basic principle of reducing our frustrations through being humble or overcoming 'the self' which is the root of our expectations and worldly ambitions is one that is compatible with carpentry work. And the logic of losing the attachment to 'the self' by connecting to the larger world around us or 'the greater whole' are principles that a good craftsperson encounters daily.

Gautama laid out a kind of code of ethics to help his followers achieve a good and happy life called 'the eightfold path'. This code consists of right understanding, right thought, right speech, right action, right livelihood, right effort, right mindfulness and right concentration. In the eightfold path, I see many similarities to the codes of good work. Carpentry trains the hand, it informs the movements and the forces needed to accomplish certain tasks. It also trains the mind and when you develop skills of the mind they translate to other aspects of your life. Carpentry has conditioned me to react more positively to life – it has taught me through repeated process that the way in which I work affects the way in which I think. I can honestly say that working with wood has made me a more confident, calmer and ultimately happier person. Those who believe the paths to spiritual understanding are restricted to temples and can only be found through meditation miss the point. Once they are present in the mind, they are present everywhere and the acts of working in the right way are in a real sense acts of meditation.

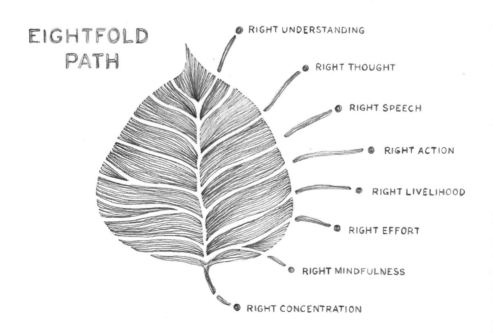

EIGHTFOLD PATH

RIGHT UNDERSTANDING

RIGHT THOUGHT

RIGHT SPEECH

RIGHT ACTION

RIGHT LIVELIHOOD

RIGHT EFFORT

RIGHT MINDFULNESS

RIGHT CONCENTRATION

The mortise and tenon joint

The mortise and tenon is both a simple and strong joint that has connected pieces of wood for thousands of years. The oldest known joint dates from early Neolithic times when it was used in the construction of wells. It has also been found joining the wooden planks of the Khufu ship, a long vessel sealed in a pit of the Giza pyramid complex from around 2500 BC. It has been found in ancient furniture from archaeological sites in the Middle East, Europe and Asia. In traditional Chinese and Japanese architecture of the Neolithic period, mortise and tenon joinery was made to interlock perfectly without glues or fastenings enabling the wood to expand and contract according to humidity. In Britain it has been used for centuries in a wide range of woodwork including the frame and panel furniture of the Middle Ages and the construction of buildings in the Tudor period. A basic mortise and tenon is comprised of two components – a square or rectangular mortise hole and the tenon tongue which fits the hole exactly. When the joint fully enters the hole, the shoulders of the tenon should be tight against the wood it joins. The joint is then glued, pinned or wedged to lock it in place. It is still one of the most common joints and for good reason – its design has lasted for thousands of years, because it works and it can be carved using basic carpentry tools. Of all the tasks in this table-making project, this will probably be the most challenging. The tools you will need to accomplish the mortise and tenon joint are as follows: pencil, marking knife, combination square, mortise gauge, mortise chisel or bevel edge chisel, wooden mallet, tenon saw, bench hook, wood glue and brush.

The mortise

There will be four mortises in each leg, which will hold the frame of the table together and there will be a mortise in each of the bottom rails connected by a central stretcher which will give the table extra strength. The first step is to decide on the depth of the mortise and mark this measurement on the edge of the mortise piece with a square. In our case it will be two thirds through the width of the leg. We mark the position of the bottom rails and aprons on the legs. The bottom rail will finish 150mm above the floor and the apron will be level with the top of the leg so that it supports the table top. Next we choose the correct chisel size. Our tenon thickness is going to be roughly a third of the thickness of the apron and rails, so the chisel you choose should be the one closest to this size. We set the two pins on our mortise gauge to the width of the mortise chisel and then set the fence of the mortise gauge to mark a mortise that is in the centre of the leg. We also need to mark the tenon shoulder marks (the tenon sides are called cheeks and the end grain faces are called shoulders). The distance between the shoulder marks is the length of the mortise. Once we have scribed the lines into our wood, we draw over them with a sharp pencil so they are easier to see.

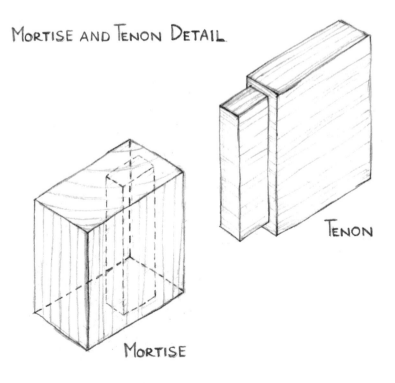

MORTISE AND TENON DETAIL

TENON

MORTISE

To cut out the mortise with a chisel, we secure the mortise piece to the bench with a clamp and use a knife to reinforce the scribed marks. Then we began to chisel out the mortise by making a number of small cuts into the wood every few millimetres. A mortise chisel is made for the job, with the extra thickness allowing the chisel to self-jig or stay on track once the mortise has started. If you are right-handed then position the leg on your right side and vice versa if you are left-handed. Your body position will help you, so try to align your body with the leg. You should be comfortable, as any tension will transfer through your body and make the job more difficult. When making the mortise hole, use a wooden mallet to hit the chisel, and don't be too shy – tentative taps will not work as well as a good clean strike. A useful tip is to start slightly away from the edge of the scribed mark, which will allow you to leverage against the walls of the mortise to help you remove the waste from the hole without fear of damaging the final walls. You should be able to use your chisel in the same direction to complete the mortise. When you have reached the required depth, you can use the chisel to cut the edges of the mortise to the marked dimensions precisely.

If you position your body correctly and you use good clean strikes, hand mortising can be very fast and accurate. If you want to use a drill driver to help you with the mortise, then use a spade bit of the same width as the mortise hole and mark the depth on the spade bit with some masking

tape so you don't drill too far. It may save you time chiselling, but it can be a little trickier to remove the waste using this method. There is also a machine called a mortiser which produces clean, square-cornered mortises by plunging a hollow chisel with an auger bit running through the centre into your wood. The auger drills as the chisel cuts – the machine is set to a repeatable position and depth so the other mortises can be cut to the same settings. This makes the mortiser faster than mortising by hand.

The tenon

There will be tenons in the aprons and rails which will join the legs together, as well as in the central stretcher which will join the bottom rails. We begin by marking the shoulder of the tenon on the face of the tenon piece. This is at the depth of our tenon and is equal to the depth of the mortise hole. We score around all four sides of the tenon piece with a knife. Then we use the mortise gauge which is still set to the width of the mortise to mark out our tenon on three sides – the face, the end grain and the non-face. Next we set the single pin on our mortise gauge to mark the shoulder size and scribe this measurement across the end grain of the tenon. Again we use a sharp pencil to go over the score lines so they are easier to see. We secure our

tenon piece in the vice at an angle so we can see the pencil lines on the face side and the end grain, then use our tenon saw to saw along the tenon cheek until we reach the depth mark. Next, we turn the wood over and repeat the process until we reach the depth mark again. Tenon saws often have a thin blade and have a brass back rib which helps to keep the saw rigid. When sawing do not force the cut, but allow the weight of the saw to cause the fine teeth to bite with each push stroke. By carefully following your scribe line and staying focused and relaxed, you can achieve near perfect results with a tenon saw.

The next job is to use the tenon saw to cut along the shoulder line on the face edge releasing the waste. We then turn the wood around to saw off the other cheek – a bench hook will help keep it in position or alternatively use a clamp or vice. To complete our tenon, again we use the single pin on our mortise gauge to mark the width of the shoulder from the end grain, down the newly cut face of the tenon. We place the tenon piece in the vice with the tenon facing upwards, carefully cut down the remaining shoulder lines with the tenon saw then again cut along the shoulder to release the waste. We now have

a tenon that is exactly the same size as our mortise. We use a bevelled chisel to neaten up the rough edges created by sawing. It is the shoulders of the tenon that once glued will do much of the work of holding the joint together, so it is vital that they are clean and square. Finally we chamfer the edges of our tenon with a block plane so they can be inserted easily. You will also need to do a dry test run with all your joints before gluing so you can be sure they fit together perfectly.

You can make tenons with just a wooden mallet and a large chisel. I find it a more satisfactory method and once you are competent at it, it is in fact faster and more accurate. However, it can be tricky if the grain of the wood is not parallel to the tenon – the potential for disaster is higher than using the tenon saw.

People also often use machines these days – a band saw or a table saw with a rip fence and a mitre fence will achieve faster results. This is especially useful if you have lots of tenons to make and it will also help you to keep all the sizes consistent. Descriptions of practical skills such as these are always difficult to read, somehow making the processes seem more complicated than they really are. You can only truly understand the joint through the hands on process and once you have accomplished your first mortise and tenon, your progress will be fast. The skills of carpentry are only improved by participating – you have to start before you can get better, so don't be scared of your work and you might surprise yourself by how fast you progress.

To understand a piece of wood, you must first grow a forest

'Nothing in the universe is contingent, but all things are conditioned to exist and operate in a particular manner by the necessity of the divine nature.'

BARUCH SPINOZA

Sometimes in life it is worth asking the questions that are the simplest or that seem the most obvious, because these are the questions that will take you closest to the truth. Since I spend much of my time as a carpenter and I concern myself with the materials of carpentry, then the simplest question I can ask myself has to be, 'what is wood?' There are different answers to this question depending on the perspective from which we are looking – the more perspectives we can look from, the more information we have and the greater our understanding. A sensible place to start is that of a definition. Wood is a porous and fibrous structural tissue found in the stems and roots of trees. It is a natural composite of cellulose fibres (which are strong in tension) embedded in a matrix of lignin (which resists compression). Even in this short description of wood there is enough information with which to improve your woodworking skills. Here is another no less valid definition of wood which considers it as a component part of the tree: wood is an evolutionary development of plants which gives structural strength to the trunk of a tree and allows it to raise its leaves high above the ground thus enabling it to compete better for the light energy which provides the food for the tree's growth through photosynthesis.

To see how something exists in its natural state is not just interesting; it is useful, as it helps us to understand something of how it wants to be. I often think of the timber I use as a square tree – if I use it in the way it was designed to exist in nature, it will usually perform better. People can sometimes lose touch with a material, forgetting the fundamentals of wood in the same way they forget what shellac is or tortoiseshell or happiness. To treat wood as if it were a tree and to ask what the tree would want is to accept that there is a greater truth outside of our definitions. Having said this, wood is a most remarkable material and it will cope outside of its environment, but to understand how to work it, to mould it, to get the most out of it, it is useful to look at what is happening structurally within the wood.

Wood is mostly made up of long, narrow longitudinal cells that align themselves with the axis of the trunk – these are what give the wood its grain. Structurally speaking wood is anisotropic, meaning it has different properties in different directions. Wood is much more resistant to compression in the same direction as the grain. As wood grows outwards, the living protoplasm inside the cells dies and deteriorates, leaving behind just the cell walls. These walls are composed mostly of cellulose fibres – the fibres are bound together with a naturally occurring polymer called lignin, a glue-like substance. Cellulose is tougher than lignin, which is why it is easier to split wood with the grain (separating the lignin) than it is to break it across the grain (separating the cellulose fibres). Not all wood is the same – Oak, for example, has a high tensile strength (resistance to forces across the grain), which is why it was traditionally used to make the heavy, horizontal beams in old buildings. I have memories of childhood days running along the thick horizontal branches of the oak tree in our local park. It had something of the impossible about it then, perhaps even more so now with my understanding of the forces involved. By observing the structural composition of a piece of wood, we can determine its 'quality' and we are better placed to decide how it should be used.

Growth rings are also a good guide to the structural qualities of timber. Wood increases in diameter by the formation of new woody layers between the existing wood and the inner bark (known as the cambium layer). This newly created wood is the sap wood which transports water and minerals from the roots to the upper parts of the tree through vessels. As new wood is formed, the inner sapwood is progressively converted to heart wood. A traverse section through a tree trunk will show concentric circles of lighter and darker wood. These rings are the annual growth rings. There may also be rays running at right angles to growth rings. These are vascular rays which are thin sheets of living tissue permeating the wood. There are differences within a growth ring – the part of the growth ring nearest the centre of the tree is formed early in the growing season. It is usually lighter in colour and is known as earlywood or springwood. The outer portion is usually known as latewood or summerwood. In softwoods, the latewood will be denser because it grows more slowly, due in part to the climate. Especially in the north, a cold winter means a tree must grow rapidly in the early summer season as soon as the temperature rises and the days are longer. Latewood usually has thick walls and small cell cavities. Since the strength is in the walls, the greater the proportion of latewood, the greater the density and strength of the wood.

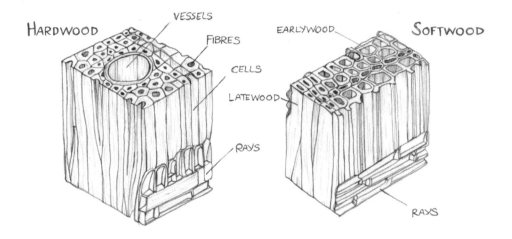

In ring-porous hardwoods like Oak and Ash, each year's growth is well defined and there is a definite relationship between the speed of growth of a tree and strength. The more rapid the tree's growth, the wider the growth rings, the heavier, harder, stronger and stiffer the wood. The latewood in ring-porous trees is usually made up of thick-walled, strength-giving fibres. As the breadth of the ring diminishes, the latewood is reduced, so that very slow growth produces comparatively light porous wood. The classifications of softwood and hardwood can be a little misleading – generally conifers are considered softwoods while wood from broad-leaved trees is hardwood, but this does not necessarily mean the wood hardness is consistent with the description. For example, Balsa is classed as a hardwood despite being very soft whereas the Yew tree is classed as softwood despite being strong and durable.

The way a tree grows is subject to its environment, the soils, its exposure to the elements and its place within a forest. A forest tree will usually make its most rapid growth in youth and decline with age. The growth rings will be larger at the centre for this reason. It also follows that since the tree is getting wider, it would need to increase its wood production year after year if the rings were to stay the same thickness. Much of a tree's design and the way it functions depends on its competition with other trees. As a tree reaches maturity and its crown becomes open, it reduces its wood production, because once a tree's leaves are capable of photosynthesis then the need to grow taller diminishes.

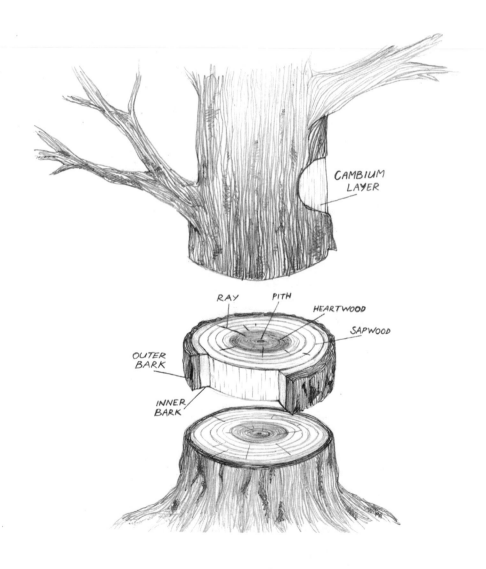

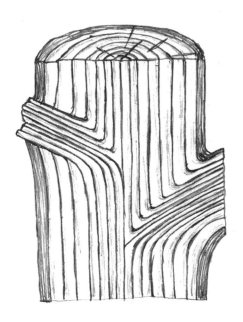

WOOD GROWTH

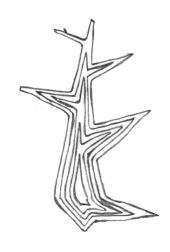

A vast amount could be written about photosynthesis – too much to go into for the purposes of this book. It is at least worth mentioning that the conversion of light energy into carbohydrate molecules such as sugar to fuel an organism is not just special, it is perhaps the greatest of all the miracles of the natural world. It is largely responsible for producing and maintaining the oxygen content of the Earth's atmosphere and supplies all of the organic compounds and most of the energy necessary for life on earth. It is the oxygenation of our planet that made the evolution of complex life possible. It is such a complex process that unlike miracles such as the eye or the brain, it has evolved just once and determining how exactly it happened is central to understanding whether life is possible on other planets. The fact that photosynthesis produces oxygen as a waste product and is largely irrelevant to the plant is always an enjoyable thought to me.

So far the explanations of wood have focused on our biological understanding of the material and the structural implications this has, but something that interests me is how wood affects the person who handles it. Carpentry doesn't work unless you follow its core principles. When the woodworker focuses on these principles and accepts the implications of biological structure, they gain a relationship with the wood and this in turn affects the way they think. There are times in my life when I have just stared at a piece of wood, all the things I have learned about this beautiful and enigmatic material will hit me all at once, I am absorbed by its inescapable gifts and I feel a kind of awe towards it. This is not an everyday experience of course, as under normal circumstances I wouldn't get much work done, but I do often wonder where the human race would be without it, or indeed 'if' the human race would be without it. The versatile powers of this material have been intertwined with human life since the beginnings of human culture and our reverence towards it is rooted as much in the spiritual as the practical.

I enjoy the ancient Greek story of the creation of the Olive tree. According to Greek mythology the Olive tree was created as a result of a contest between Poseidon, god of the sea, and Athena, goddess of wisdom and war (and patron of the arts and crafts). The contest was to ultimately decide who would become the protector of a great new city in Attica (the region that became Greece). The city would be named after the god or goddess who would deliver the most useful and divine gift. Poseidon struck the hard rock of the Acropolis with his trident causing water to rush out and thereby creating a spring of salt water. Athena followed by striking a rock with her spear to produce a humble Olive tree. The recognition of the tree's value in producing wood to construct houses and boats, oil that provided food, medicine, preservatives and fuel for lamps, as well as the olives themselves, resulted in Athena winning the contest and thus Athens was born. The legend is also a symbol of a change in Greek history, of supplanting aggression for a life that is closely bound to the cultivation of the land and a peaceful existence rooted in domesticity and intellectual wisdom.

The significance of wood to human life runs deeper still than even thousands of years of ancestral history. There is something strange and unconscious that happens when working with wood that I find difficult to explain, something I feel intuitively, a relationship that exists not with the intellect but within the instinctive movements of the hand. I have thought a great deal about this over the years: why wood feels so familiar, the dimensions so comfortable and comforting, its soft firmness assuring and reassuring. Part of it is the familiarity of a craftsperson using a material day in, day out, but it is more than this – the feeling was present before I learned the skills of carpentry.

At the start of this section, I said it was important to not forget what wood is; it is just as important to not forget what we are and where we have come from. Understanding our connection to wood reaches its conclusion in the origins of our relationship to it. There is an early species of small, nocturnal, arboreal mammal called *Carpolestes simpsoni* that differs from the other early shrew-like mammals. It is significant because it had grasping digits instead of claws – these grasping digits were because it had ventured into the trees. It is believed that this creature was the ancestor of all primates and this was the lineage that led directly to the hominins, the closest relatives of *Homo sapiens*. Many consider *Homo habilis* to be the first representative of modern humankind because of its capacity for handling tools. *Homo habilis* kept some of the skeletal characteristics of their ancestors that had made them great climbers and probably spent considerable time in trees, foraging, sleeping and avoiding predators. Importantly, they were the first of our relatives to have opposable thumbs. The ability to manipulate the world around us and develop the complex and wonderful mind of the modern human being is in part a consequence of our relationship to trees.

There is a reason why the hand becomes comfortable and unconscious when working with wood. It is because wood is not only a material which we have evolved with, it is the material which has caused us to evolve. The tree has shaped our bodies, our hands, our minds and subsequently our thoughts and in this sense, when we are working with wood, it is hard to resist the conclusion that we are in some way in a relationship with our creator, whatever your understanding of that may be.

CARPOLESTES SIMPSONI

Base assembly: the essential rules never change

Our job for the day at Darley Barn is to assemble the base of my table. All the component parts are now complete, cut to the correct lengths, the mortise and tenons have been cleaned and the potentially difficult to reach sections of the wood have been sanded down. The first task is to put together the trestles and check the joint positions with a dry run. We do this because, as with the table top, if a joint does not fit, it would be an unfortunate and messy procedure to adjust it once the glue is applied. There are a few minor adjustments to the widths of the mortises, but the depths are all good and once together, the shoulders of the tenons are flat against the mortise pieces. It is important not to rush in the anticipation to see your table come together. You need to be perfectly happy with all the joints before moving on to the gluing stage because the quality of the joints and how they fit together will have a substantial bearing on the lifespan of your table.

Next it is time to clamp up, so we adjust the pins on the sash clamps to a width slightly wider than that of the trestles, leaving enough room for two thin blocks of wood which will protect the wood of the legs. Similar to the table-top gluing, we have clamps above and below the trestles so they will not 'pop out' under the pressure once the clamps are tightened. We apply PVA glue liberally to the mortise and tenon joints and to the tenon shoulders with a brush before tightening the clamps, again adjusting each clamp a little at a time so the pressure is spread evenly.

Trestle Assembly

At this point we use a large square to check if the trestles are parallel and square. This is especially important for the trestles because any twists or distortions in the legs will be easily noticeable and could result in one of life's greatest irritants – the wobbly eating table. Once it is all clamped up, we carefully and thoroughly clean the wood of all excess glue with a damp cloth. We obviously don't want any glue to be seen, but even small amounts of glue that dries clear will still resist the oils and waxes of the finish coats and it could look unsightly. Because of the cold conditions, we take the precaution of using a heater to be sure the PVA will set properly. A perfect temperature is above 15 degrees, but below 5 degrees Celsius, PVA ceases to be effective and the joint would be weak or defective. Ideally we wanted to get the whole base clamped up by the end of the day. Although PVA can dry fast in hot conditions, it will take a couple of hours to set properly especially in these temperatures, so we take a longer lunch than usual. In the afternoon we cautiously remove the clamps from the trestles. There is always a feeling of trepidation that surrounds gluing in colder temperatures, but thankfully they had set correctly.

The next job is to join the two trestles together by attaching the long aprons and the bottom stretcher. This job is relatively straightforward in principle, but it can be tricky to get it perfectly square and clamping it together with protective wooden blocks can be

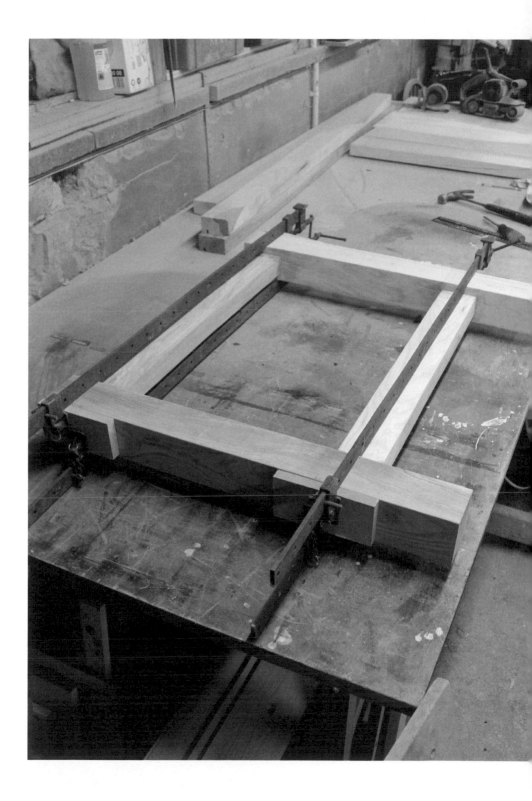

a little unwieldy especially on your own. In such a case masking tape can act as a helpful extra hand. If it is proving difficult, the benefits of a flat, level surface will reveal themselves immediately. Again, a dry run is necessary, mainly to see how the joints fit, but also to test how long it will take to assemble. On a hot day you may have less than 10 minutes to glue all the component parts so you want to be sure you can do it in time. Since the workshop floor is a little bumpy in parts, we put down a large sheet of MDF. On a flat surface, the legs of our trestles are wide enough to stand alone which helps matters. We attach the first long apron by pushing the mortise and tenon joints together and follow with the second long apron. Finally we splay out the trestles from the bottom and push the low stretcher into place. If necessary you can knock the joints together lightly using your mallet and a block of wood. If your mortise and tenon joints are made correctly they should be tight, but there should be some give in the joints which allows enough movement for assembly. Remember also that the strength in joints is largely due to the glue, so if the mortise and tenons need to be forced together then there is a chance the joints might eventually be glue starved.

It is also a good idea to clamp it together on the dry run. Our sash clamps are not long enough to reach the length of the table on their own, so

BASE ASSEMBLY

we join two of them together (which is normal practice), but the last thing you want to be doing is scrambling around trying to join clamps together and then adjusting them after you have applied the glue.

Once we are confident that the table can be assembled with no problems, we proceed to the gluing stage. Again, always check that you have all the necessary tools before gluing begins – clamps set to the right length, wood blocks cut, and it might sound obvious, but check you have enough glue in your bottle and you have a damp cloth at the ready to clean all the surfaces of glue immediately after the table is secured together. We apply the glue and clamp the table using the same procedure as the dry run. It can be difficult to square up a table using just a square for various reasons. For example, sometimes the clamps can put the aprons under pressure and temporarily bow them slightly. It is therefore best to square up the table by measuring it diagonally from corner to corner and adjusting it until the measurements are equal. A good tip is to use the clamps to help you with this. If the measurements are not the same, you can adjust the skew of the clamp to press in on the longer of the two measurements.

We again leave the table for a few hours and use the heater to be sure the glue will set. The table has thankfully assembled with no significant problems. As so often is the case in carpentry, your preparation for the main event is the difference between success and failure. Assembly is all about following the simple rules, because the simple rules don't change. Your success is really a culmination of the

work you have done previously. Being organised before the gluing stage will undoubtedly help you, but the true preparation goes right through the job. From making the correct-sized mortise and tenons so they fit together properly, to measuring and cutting the correct-sized aprons, rails and stretcher. You could even go right back to the beginning when our wood was still a tree, for example, our decision to mark the straightest grained section for the legs to ensure they would not twist or bow in the drying process as some of the other wood did. All of these factors and decisions contribute to the success of the assembly and they all help to avoid the build-up of minor discrepancies that can make life difficult. A millimetre out on some of the lengths, a slightly offset mortise, a tiny bow in the legs and before you know it, your table is out of square and you are left struggling to find the culprit and get the table back into shape. It is now displaying the qualities of a single table and it feels as though we have made it through the last of the stages that have the potential for disaster. I feel confident now that the table top would go on but of course until that moment is here, we can't allow ourselves the luxury of relaxing too much.

Confessions of a carpenter

'It's what you learn after you know it all that counts.'

JOHN WOODEN

As your skills as a woodworker improve, you will become more familiar with recognising good workmanship, but this also means you will recognise the bad. This can be a frustrating time. Work that you had once considered excellent you may now think of as ordinary and work that you had once considered perfectly acceptable you may now see as wholly unacceptable. However, these are all signs that you are a more competent carpenter and the dissatisfaction of your work may just be the evidence of progress.

Part of improving your carpentry involves becoming aware of where you are going wrong and learning to understand how to adjust your behaviour to make your work better. Becoming a better carpenter is not just about improving your skills, it also involves reducing the number of errors you make. I have noticed in my time working with others that some people have a tendency to repeat the same mistakes, over and over again. It is not necessarily because they are careless by nature, but sometimes it feels as though they are almost trying too hard, as if rushing towards their goals.

When I am training people, if someone makes a mistake, I ask them to try to acknowledge the mistake. Not in a condescending way (at least I hope not); I ask them to admit it to me, yes, but more importantly, I want them to admit it to themselves. Maybe a joint doesn't fit, glue hasn't set, a surface has been damaged because a blade should have been sharpened or a dimension is wrong because of an imperial to metric translation. In such circumstances it is common in the workplace to simply push ahead to amend a problem usually in an attempt to catch up on time. But without fully understanding what has happened, the same mistake can be repeated, which potentially loses you far more time.

To find the root of the error requires some thought. You will need to trace it back to its source, like a detective going progressively through events to find their carpentry culprit. Even if the mistake is a minor one, it is useful to try and analyse it in a similar way to a major one, though this is easier said than done of course. If one of your table legs has been cut way too short rendering it useless, you would certainly question how this has happened, but even when the cut is wrong for a temporary spacer or support, I will still find out why. A common measuring mistake, for example, is cutting 1,010mm instead of 1,100mm. Recognising this means you take extra care with these types of numbers when it matters, especially when you are tired. Taking the time to analyse the insignificant error can therefore reduce the potential for a substantial error later on.

As we delve deeper into our flaws they become more difficult to decipher or even recognise.

I remember having to admit to myself that I had used my powered palm router to avoid others knowing that my chisel skills were not good enough. This kind of response to life is not for the faint hearted as it requires a certain degree of courage and humility. I have known confident carpenters who did not seem to progress as well as they should have. They reached a point whereby their work functioned well enough, but they never seemed to achieve the heights their bravado had reached, for – I suppose – in the end they just stopped learning. Perhaps it is a resistance to accept flaws, a reluctance to face up to weakness or even a fear to see anything negative. I think with regards to learning, there can be a tendency to over exert positive thinking. For me the answer is to not focus too much on either the positive or the negative, just to try and see the truth and adjust to this. It is being honest about our mistakes in life and recognising our ignorance about a subject that allows us to become better people.

Perhaps the most famous example of accepting ignorance in order to progress is the charismatic figure of Socrates, and it wouldn't feel right not to have him make an appearance in a book such as this. It is said that the oracle at Delphi had been asked who the wisest man in the world was, to which the oracle replied that there was no one wiser than Socrates. Socrates did not agree with this given that he was certain of his own ignorance and set out to prove the oracle wrong. But after discussing the matter with many Athenians he found that even amongst the most learned people he knew, their knowledge was limited or indeed false. He came to the conclusion that he was the wisest man at least in Athens, not because of what he knew, but because he understood what he did not know. This type of logical humility can also exist on a more spiritual dimension by helping us to reinterpret our understanding of the 'self'. The Japanese philosopher Hajime Tanabe said that 'to philosophize, first one must confess'. The roots of this idea go back to a branch of Buddhism known as Pure Land Buddhism. He claimed that the confession of our ignorance leads to 'absolute nothingness' and to self-awakening and wisdom. Like Socrates, he considered that the task of philosophy is to understand what we are, and for this reason we must continually examine our lives, using philosophy as a way to relate to our true self.

Whether it is cutting an insignificant block of wood or addressing a spiritual crisis, the confession is the beginning of the solution. I can also

remember confessing to myself that I really wasn't enjoying my life and that my job that was getting me down. This may sound a little strange, but I can remember saying it out loud to myself, as if hearing the words made it more real. If it was real then it gave me the power to perceive it and thus I would have the ability to change it. I had always aspired to work for myself, to do something more creative that I felt had meaning. This confession gave me the impetus to make a change and it was the catalyst to me leaving my job and turning to woodwork and writing.

Ultimately to be considered a master craftsperson, you must be familiar with these processes, because it is confessing that allows you to teach yourself. The master craftsperson must become receptive to their own mistakes, they should instruct themselves, they should be aware of what they need to practise in order to progress. This is how they continually improve and in this there is a lesson for us in the wider aspects of our lives. The ability to recognise our flaws is valuable in life. To confess a limitation is a means to improve it. If you have the courage to admit what you are, you will have the courage to become who you should be. We should all remember to never stop learning – it is the learning of new things and the ability to change and develop which helps to keep our spirits alive. The more we learn, the more we connect to the world, the more we expand the limits of our minds and the less we concern ourselves with unimportant things. This is the path to becoming a wiser and more fulfilled person.

Left: Socrates

Table top mounting

It was my last day for a while in Darley Barn workshop. The new morning was misty, rendering the views with a frosty haze like the cloud of an underdeveloped photograph. There was still a thin coating of snow on the ground but this time it was hard and icy. There had been so many weather conditions up here in the Peak District, but I had expected as much. The only condition the weather had yet to try was warmth. I was looking forward to the spring now. In fact I rather yearned for it, but that's what is good about the seasons of the north. They seem to last just the right length of time for you to feel tired of them and then they change – as though we have somewhat reluctantly tuned to their rhythms. But my mood was one of hopeful anticipation because this was the day I will see my table together, in one piece.

Attaching the table top to the base is more complicated than just fixing it with screws or gluing it down. As we have discussed, wood is a hygroscopic material that will continually gain or lose water in order to balance to the moisture content of the surrounding air. This in turn means the wood will expand or contract and attaching the top without allowing for this wood movement can result in the table splitting or cracking. For this reason, we use buttons or table fasteners which are designed to accommodate this wood movement. These are screwed into the underside of the table top and then sit within grooves in the aprons. They can ride in these grooves as the top expands and contracts while still holding the top to the base. There are steel versions of buttons which you can buy to save time and there is also something called a desk fastener which looks like a figure of eight. One half of the figure of eight is screwed into the underside of the table top, while the other half is screwed into a recess in the apron. As the table top expands and contracts the fastener pivots around the screw. A biscuit jointer can also potentially be used, but it can be difficult to get everything lined up correctly.

I think it more fitting to the project to make our own buttons – using our Ash offcuts would look the best and would react to any change in conditions in a similar way to the rest of the table. Making the buttons is a relatively simple procedure; we start by ripping a piece of our left over Ash into a long strip which has a cross section of 5cm x 3cm. When making your buttons, you want these small pieces to have as much strength as possible, so make sure the grain does not run up and down, or the short grain will break off under any pressure. The buttons need to have a tongue which will sit perfectly within the groove of the apron. To make this, we set the fence of the table saw to make a groove in our strip equal to the distance from the top of the table apron to the apron groove. Then we simply create the tongue of the button by setting the height of the table saw to remove the waste. Making any small parts using power tools, especially a table saw, is dangerous; the procedure always involves making the component part from a larger piece of wood, then cutting the individual pieces from this larger piece. In the case of our buttons, we simply cut our strip into individual pieces 4cm in width, which means our buttons are now 5cm x 4cm x 3cm including the tongue. The last stage of our button making is to drill a pilot hole and counter sink through the thick part so that the button will not split when it is screwed into the table top.

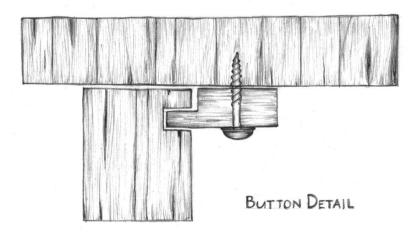

BUTTON DETAIL

Often buttons would be placed only on the two sides perpendicular to the direction of the grain. This is because the most significant movement in the wood is across the grain, so the slide of the buttons in the grooves will be most beneficial in this direction. In our case we want to avoid any cupping in our table top so we decide to use the buttons on all sides to stop it from going out of shape. We had always considered this a possibility because it is a reasonably large table and the drying time of our wood had been pushed to its minimum, but there should still be enough flexibility in the fasteners to avoid any splits or cracks. Depending on how bad the cupping in a table top you can also plane or sand it flat again. If the cupping or warping is serious and it is not possible to plane or sand flat again without it resulting in thin edges or a thin middle, the best strategy is to cut the boards apart at the seams, re-joint them and glue up the table top again. Bear in mind each cut will subtract the 3mm blade from the width of your table top, so this will only work if you have enough material to spare.

Next we spread a protective blanket over the sheet of MDF (which is our flat surface to assemble on) to avoid damaging our table top. We turn the table top upside down and lay it on the blanket; we also turn the base upside down and place it on the underside of the table top. We carefully measure the distances to the edges of the table top to ensure the base is perfectly in the centre. We insert a button into one of our apron grooves and screw it into the table top with a suitable length screw (screwing through the table top at this late stage would of course be highly vexing). We repeat the process for the other buttons. In total there are ten buttons, three on each of the long sides and two on each of the short. All that remains is to flip the whole table around onto its legs to reveal the finished article.

This last stage of the assembly process went fast. The table is not as yet finished – the wood is still in quite a raw state and it will need sanding and waxing, but there it is standing before my eyes. It is often the case that the end phase of a job gives the greatest reward, but it is the work at the beginning that allows these fruits of labour. There is also a sense of relief seeing all those component parts finally acting together as one, and I leave the workshop to return home in a buoyant mood knowing there will be a functioning table waiting for me on my return.

Inside the forest, outside the mind

'There is no repose like that of the green deep woods.'

JOHN MUIR

Every year, I try to remove myself from the world of deadlines and duty, to indulge myself in the simple unsophisticated pleasure of the woodland walk. Spring is finally here, maybe not quite yet in Darley Dale but it has shown its face in London. I read once that spring travels north at walking pace, which is always a pleasant thought. There is enchantment in all seasons of the forest, whether the frozen magic of winter, the abundant glory of summer or the poignant beauty of the autumn, but spring is my favourite time to walk among the trees, experiencing the hard-earned celebratory joy of nature emerging from the cold. I like the English word 'spring' – most languages use a word derived from early or fore to describe this time of year, but spring seems to catch the spark of energy and cheer.

There are, of course, many varieties of forest around the world depending on the climate, but most people are aware of the three main groups. The northern Boreal forests of Conifers form a continuous tract of trees around the whole globe wherever there is land from the Atlantic coast of North America to the Pacific shores of Alaska, across the Bering Strait and through Siberia into Scandinavia. The equatorial tropical rainforests of West Africa, South east Asia and South America house a staggering number of tall tree species – true ancient forests that have made use of the perfect growing conditions for tens of millions of years. Finally, there are the temperate, predominantly deciduous, broad-leaved forests of North America, North east Asia and Europe that have evolved to react and shift with four well-defined seasons.

What people are often less aware of are the more specific conditions within these groups. In the British Isles, for example, there is an incredible variety of woodland landscapes each sustaining their own particular combinations of dependent fauna and flora. The lowland Beech and Yew woodlands with their towering smooth grey trees in the limestone and chalk soils of southeast England or the ancient mixed deciduous woods of Wales with their carpets of vegetation. The native Scots Pine woodlands of the Grampians, relics from the Scandinavian Boreal forests housing charismatic wildlife such as the crossbill with its specialist feeding tool and the capercaillie with its glass bottle call. There are the hardy upland Birch woods with their understorey of Juniper that survive the infertile soils and harsh weather conditions of the Highlands and provide an invaluable habitat for the rare pearl-bordered fritillary butterfly and the aspen hoverfly. The upland Oak woods of north and west Britain with their rich gardens of mosses, ferns and lichens that drape garlands over statuesque tree trunks and support hole-nesting birds such as wood warblers, redstarts and pied flycatchers. Or the ancient wet woodlands in the fens of East Anglia and the flood plains of the New Forest, rich in invertebrates such as the rare crane fly and the netted carpet moth which subsequently support the feeding of pipistrelle and noctule bats.

We don't always need to be in the depths of the countryside to enjoy the woodland walk – the environments that are connected to our communities such as the wood pastures and parklands of country houses or gardens are an essential part of the British landscape, as are the urban woods that lie within or on the outskirts of our cities – areas such as Richmond Park in southwest London which supports foxes, deer and a huge variety of beetles and butterfly. These environments have usually been managed for hundreds of years which can be a good thing. For example, they can often be interspersed with open areas of grassland, heathland or woodland wildflowers and it is not uncommon to have pollarded trees that are of a great age which is good for mosses and lichen. They are an important way to bring wildlife to the community, offering a chance for the city dweller to experience and connect with nature. To see the bright flash of a green woodpecker flying close by or to witness the majesty of Britain's largest mammal, the red deer, are encounters that can stay with the urban mind forever.

I have my own particular escapes which I frequent, one of which is Highgate Wood in northwest London. Just to the north is Queen's Wood and just to the south is Highgate Cemetery which is the final resting place for many a well-known figure including philosopher Karl Marx, writer Douglas Adams, scientist Michael Faraday and the poet Christina Rossetti. I took myself through all three this year for my annual springtime hiatus.

I waited for a good weather forecast and took an early underground train to Highgate in an attempt to miss the crowds. A short walk north from Highgate station are the carved metal gates of the entrance at which I left my troubles for the next few hours. The early morning spring sun was low in the sky and the tree shadows seemed to stretch as far as the eye could see. We often consider expansive landscapes of snow-capped mountains or cascading waterfalls to be the pinnacle of beauty in the natural world, but when I am on these early morning woodland walks, immersed in nature, I often think to myself, this is one of the finest sights I can ever remember.

I had read a great deal about wood since this whole process had begun. I certainly had more knowledge, but to understand anything in life properly, you have to see it in its natural environment, like visiting a foreign friend in their home country or seeing your docile family cat hunting live prey. To see a tree in the environment it had evolved, not just as part of a boundary to a

field or in a well-kept public park, but as part of a wood, was to make real the words and pictures of theory. Even the simplest processes of nature make more sense when you are a witness to them. For example, we all know that plants need light to survive, but it is not until you stand within the dimmed, filtered light of a wood and look straight up towards the sky that you begin to feel something of the struggle to capture the sun's energy.

Once you begin to see the workings of nature, it is only a matter of time before your vision expands and connects to others. It is as if you begin to hear and understand a whole new language that you had been previously unaware of. The language of a wood is quietly spoken and the subtleties of a woodland ecosystem only reveal themselves to those who tread softly. Slowly the details begin to emerge, details that are always there but are invisible to the hurried walker. The bracken and ferns pushing their way through the earth and uncurling themselves, the delicate pale purple petals of dog violets hiding in the grasses (the origin of the term shrinking violets), the bright yellow heads of sulphur tufts feeding on the rotting wood of an old Oak. A gently decaying fallen tree providing sustenance for beetles and shelter for small mammals, around which the fresh leaves of keen young saplings make use of the extra light through the canopy. And these are only the visible functions of the forest; there is a whole world of processes taking place out of sight in other microscopic dimensions.

Recent discoveries about complex connections of the forest have expanded our understanding of tree life and they have forced us to re-evaluate our perceptions of the forest ecosystem. Trees are no longer the simple, slow-growing, benign structures that we had previously thought. They are in fact much more dynamic, able to react quickly to the world around them. A young Oak, for example, will send messages from one leaf under insect attack and pass it on to other leaves. A similar tactic is used by many other trees – a Beech tree if threatened by roe deer can very quickly increase the tannin content in its leaves, so they become bitter and less palatable to dissuade the hungry visitor. Sometimes the tree will not only respond to the surrounding environment, but actively change it for its own purposes. A Pine forest has a cunning defence if attacked by aphids – it will send out an invisible cloud of perfume which attracts ladybirds and just like a shark attracted to blood, the ladybirds will follow the scent from miles around to locate their prey.

One of the most important aspects of functioning woodland is the fungi, without which the energy from the trees would not be recycled and the tough woody matter would not replenish the soil. Some fungi start the process while the trees are living, like the honey fungus and bracket fungus that dwell within the trees and weaken them over time. Others get to work on dead wood such as wet rot fungus or jelly fungus which feed on the cellulose and lignin converting them into softer tissue. Their growth within the wood helps other detritivores (creatures that feed on dead organic material) such as bacteria and beetle larvae to gain access. Gradually as the wood becomes more penetrated and open, invertebrates such as woodlice and millipedes can take over.

Some of these fungi run through the earth for miles, their long threads known as hyphae (networks of which are called mycelium) searching for dead wood to break down, making it available for the trees to feed on, recycling at its finest. In some forests, a special type of fungus known as mycorrhizal fungi attaches itself to fine roots that extend into the soil and covers them completely like a sock. A mutually beneficial exchange takes place – the fungus is able to obtain sugars that the tree produces using photosynthesis while in return the fungus provides the plant with vital nutrients that it extracts from the soil. Some of these fungi can join with lots of different types of trees. If a connected tree that has this fungus on its roots is being attacked by an insect, it can send a message to any number of other trees. Not only can they communicate, but they can also send nutrients to other trees and share food. It is no longer sufficient to think of trees as individuals – each of them are living as part of a network of organisms within the forest. These associated networks have evolved over hundreds of millions of years but we are only at the beginning of understanding the complexities of the forest ecosystem. For me, knowing about these multifarious nuances of connection enriches the forest further and makes it ever more compelling.

You never leave a wood feeling worse than when you entered it. The sheer magnificence of the place drags the weariest of souls towards the light. The requisite condition to receive the counselling of the woods is passivity – when you yield to the woods, your senses open and become the guiding force of your thoughts. When the senses are active, the body feels more. Breathe deeply and smell the fresh new stems that burst through the musk of rotting wood or the garlic of the ramson or Jack-by-the-hedge when the leaves are broken. Slowly meander and pause for a moment to listen to the distinct gently smothered sound of the forest. The gossip of a blackcap warble floating beyond the hard cackle of a jay and, high above, the sway of the canopy leaves swishing like a distant ocean in the sky. There is no imagination required – it is all here in real form and the beauty can be quite arresting. The bright translucent foliage of a thousand greens, contrasting against the thick dark vertical columns of bark, the wisps of cool light catching the delicate dew-sprayed textures of the forest flora making it glisten and sparkle out of the dark undergrowth. At times it feels almost too perfect, as though it has all been carefully designed. But I suppose this is the point – the woods feel natural to us because they are natural to us. By this I mean that they are deeply ingrained in our consciousness. When humans first arrived on the British Isles, the whole land would have been covered in ancient woodland. We have evolved to perceive an idea of beauty through looking at the colour combinations and textures of nature and to be around the natural world makes us feel happier and healthier.

In Japan they have a practice called '*shinrin-yoko*', which translates as forest bathing. It was a phrase coined by the Japanese forestry ministry in 1982 when being in the presence of trees became part of a national public health programme to encourage preventative health care and healing. Woodlands are a huge part of Japanese culture and the modern programme was almost certainly influenced by the once dominant Shinto religion which is rooted in the worship of nature with folk tales that are alive with the spirits of the forest. There are numerous Japanese and South Korean studies that have established a robust body of scientific research on the health benefits of spending time under the canopy of a forest. Their claims include a boost to the immune system, reduction of the stress hormone cortisol, enhancement of mental awareness and a lower blood pressure. There is also interesting research that suggests a physical link between the air in a forest and the improvement of health. Trees and plants give off various essential oils generally called phytoncides which are emitted to protect them from germs and insects. The inhalation of these supports and improves our immune systems. At times the science feels a little amorphous, but whether all the claims are true is personally not important to me. Regardless, I can feel something good that happens from being in a forest – maybe it is just the sense of peace that comes from being able to appreciate nature, but this is enough for me. Perhaps the reasons are just too intricate to prove or disprove, but I don't need proof of happiness. The feeling I have from a forest is sufficient to know that we should protect these landscapes not only for the preservation of the wildlife that relies on them, but for our own sense of well-being.

There is another sensation that is the companion of these arboreal wanderings, one that has a spiritual power. If I had to choose a word to describe it, it might be melancholy, but the British use of this term always seems a little too sad and doesn't capture the poignancy of the feeling. Forever present in the forest is the beautiful paradox of ephemeral permanence – the transient existence of passing organisms within an ancient framework of centuries made solid. Trees outlive us, they make real our impermanence and confront our sense of mortality, but at the same time we see these

great monuments of time undergoing the same natural processes as we do. Within the forest, there is life and death in equal measure where growth and decay infinitely interconnect. To witness this gracious dance of creation and destruction before our eyes helps us to remember what is important in life. It allows us to emerge from a long forest walk with the clarity and clear air of new perspective.

I leave Highgate Wood by the afternoon and before I go home, I walk south through Highgate Cemetery. I want to visit the grave of Christina Rossetti, the poet. I had recently read a poem of hers that I enjoyed and I had brought the poem with me. When I eventually found the grave, I thought I might have taken a photograph, but it felt wrong to stand in her place of rest and record the monument of her death; better to show a record of her life. I decided to quietly read out the poem which captures something of the woodland walk. I think her ghost would have appreciated it.

The Trees' Counselling

I was strolling sorrowfully
Thro' the cornfields and the meadows;
The stream sounded melancholy,
And I walked among the shadows;
While the ancient forest trees
Talked together in the breeze;
In the breeze that waved and blew them,
With a strange weird rustle thro' them.
Said the oak unto the others
In a leafy voice and pleasant:
"Here we all are equal brothers,
"Here we have nor lord nor peasant.
"Summer, Autumn, Winter, Spring,
"Pass in happy following.
"Little winds may whistle by us,
"Little birds may overfly us;
"But the sun still waits in heaven
"To look down on us in splendour;
"When he goes the moon is given,
"Full of rays that he doth lend her:
"And tho' sometimes in the night
"Mists may hide her from our sight,

"She comes out in the calm weather,
"With the glorious stars together."
From the fruitage, from the blossom,
From the trees came no denying;
Then my heart said in my bosom:
"Wherefore are though sad and sighing?
"Learn contentment from this wood
"That proclaimeth all states good;
"Go not from it as it found thee;
"Turn thyself and gaze around thee."
And I turned: behold the shading
But showed forth the light more clearly;
The wild bees were honey-lading;
The stream sounded hushing merely,
And the wind not murmuring
Seemed, but gently whispering:
"Get thee patience; and thy spirit
"Shall discern in all things merit."

Christina Georgina Rossetti

Part 4
Table
Finishing

Planing and sanding

I had seen a part of all four seasons in the making of my table, mostly due to the time needed for the drying process. We are now in the home straight and this visit is the last leg of my experience. Spring has walked north to Darley Dale, the buds are showing, and the birds are celebrating the shadowy morning light with the first of the year's dawn choruses. I had travelled the previous evening and had woken early to radio headlines of an overnight 11 per cent crash in the Dow Jones stock market. As I walked across this landscape towards the workshop, the sun rising to the east, the moon falling to the west, the great heavenly dance of the cosmos before my eyes, I wondered if I had ever cared less about a news story in all my life.

Robbie had covered the table with a blanket to combat the unsurmountable temptation of placing a cup of tea on its bare surface. The removal of the blanket feels like an unveiling – it is nice to see my table again. To my eyes it is looking good. To some extent the finishing process had already begun, the high spots of the table top had been planed down before mounting and some hand sanding of the trestles had taken place before base assembly. It is now time for a thorough sanding and we begin by using a belt sander with a course 40 grit. The coarseness of abrasive paper commonly referred to as sandpaper is determined by the size of the abrasive particles bonded to the paper. The grade is a measure of the number of particles that will fit in a centimetre, so a 100-grit abrasive paper is equal to 100 particles per square centimetre. This coarseness can range from as low as 20 grit to as high as 1,200 grit depending on the type of abrasive paper.

A general guide is to use a grit of 40–60 for heavy sanding, a grit of 80–120 for removing small imperfections, and for finishing smoothly or polishing a surface, work towards a grit of 220. Timber that requires a very fine finish such as French polish will be sanded with over 360 grit.

Sandpaper is supplied in roll, disc or sheet form depending on how it will be used. Sandpaper is not the best description for these abrasive sheets since they are not in fact sand at all. The term goes back to a time when cabinet makers of the day would make their own sandpapers by coating old paper with animal glues and dipping them into sand. These abrasive papers nowadays come in a variety of forms. Glass or flint, which are among the oldest kinds of abrasives used on raw wood, are usually cheap and wear out quickly, but will do the job. Garnet paper, which is popular with cabinet makers, has a good bite and lasts a long time. Aluminium oxide, made from metallic oxide coatings, clog quickly but are especially suited to power sanders due to their long-lasting qualities. And finally, silicon carbide are extremely fine and 'cut' well when used on fine finishing work. There are also other non-paper types of abrasives on the market usually for very fine polishing. They are also sometimes used in removing stains or for reviving wood and include pumice powders, rottenstone, French chalk, Vienna chalk, steel wool and a plethora of waxes and creams.

Sanding by hand will give you a greater degree of control, but the price you pay for this control is the hard slog of labour. For this reason, powered sanders have become quite standard in the workshop and have to some degree even changed the table-making process itself. The table maker of yesteryear would have hand planed each part to exact dimensions before assembly. These days a table maker can work rougher and smooth the table once final assembly is completed. In the right hands a belt sander is a wonderful machine that saves countless hours of labour, but in the wrong hands it is deceptively destructive and the smallest of lapses in concentration can result in undesirable wells in a previously beautiful table top. The most important technique when using a belt sander is to keep it moving at all times. The belt should spin in the same direction as the grain of the wood but you should keep the machine moving back and forth across the grain. This is especially important at the beginning of the process when the course grit of the sandpaper can do most harm. When we are levelling and smoothing, we are trying to take the whole of the table top down, not just the sections that need work. A good tip is to draw chalk or pencil lines onto the surface, which will keep your sanding consistent. The marks will also help if you get disturbed or need a break as you can return to the job knowing where you have previously sanded. For us, this preliminary belt sanding takes a couple of hours of non-stop work before we are happy the table is level and smooth. With all sanding there is the inevitable production of fine dust particles. The belt sander should have a built-in extraction bag, but nevertheless, of all the jobs in the workshop it is desirable to wear a dust mask. At this point some discrepancies in the wood become apparent, though the table is mostly in good shape because we had tried to choose the best wood throughout the process. There is, however, one slightly sunken knot in the table top which will need a little work.

To fill the hole we use a beeswax-based coloured filler. Some of the wax sticks you can purchase are applied by melting the wax with a heat gun, but I find the beeswax-based ones especially convenient. I usually melt them with a lighter or simply rub or push them into the hole or scratch which needs repair. Our first step is to determine the colour; I had purchased a selection of mid to dark waxes for this purpose – the closest colour is described as Tudor brown. Bear in mind that if you cannot find a colour to match your wood, it is perfectly possible to make your own filler by adding a natural pigment such as burnt umber to beeswax and mixing them together with a little turpentine or linseed oil. We use a flexible knife to push the wax into place; a spatula or credit card will also do the job, and

once filled we smooth the area of any excess wax. Finally, we apply another thin layer of coloured wax and continue with the sanding process.

Next, we move to the random orbital sander. This is a versatile machine that consists of an abrasive disc held in position usually with a Velcro pad. It can be used for coarse sanding but it is also excellent for polishing if a finer grade of abrasive disc is used. The random orbital movement was introduced to avoid the tell-tale cross-circular whorls of the rotary disc sander. We start with a 140-grit disc and gradually work our way through the grades until we reach 220. Patience plays a part in all sanding and using the random orbital sander is no exception. It can be tempting to exert pressure to speed things up a little, but you should allow the weight of the machine and the friction of the paper to do the work.

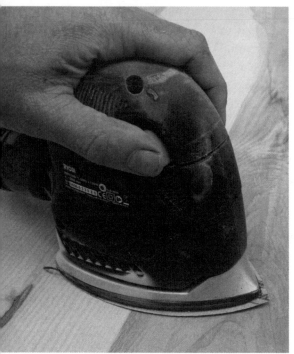

How far you take the sanding process really depends on personal preference. Many a novice carpenter will sand as an afterthought and a quick once over is enough to satisfy them. Even seasoned table makers can find the sanding process rather tiresome, which results in a somewhat neglected job. It can take a while to understand the importance of sanding to the final finish. If your table looks good, it is easy to believe that the process has reached its conclusion, but it is surprising just how much more of the wood's beauty is waiting to be revealed. I sometimes like to imagine what is happening on a microscopic dimension, each pass of a higher grade smoothing the lumps and bumps of the wood further, allowing the light to reflect evenly from its surface. I try to participate, to invite time into the process and to enjoy the gradual revelation of deeper grain detail and colour.

Finally, we go over the whole piece again by hand with a fine sandpaper; table sanding should always involve some sort of finishing by hand. This gets you down to the wood's level, it brings you into contact with the wood, and what the hand touches the eye is more in tune with. You may, of course, wish to do the whole sanding process by hand and this does have its advantages. Besides being quieter, it tends to produce less dust and it is easier to get into the hard to reach places. When sanding by hand you should always use a sanding block. This not only makes it easier to use, but it also sands more evenly by bridging the gap between inconsistencies. Without a sanding block, your hand will simply follow the contours of the wood. You can buy ready-made sanding blocks which are often just plywood with a piece of cork glued to one side (this makes it more comfortable to work with) but we made ours from offcuts in the workshop. Again, we work in the same direction as the grain, methodically from one part to the next so we don't miss any areas of the table.

The very last stage is to sand all the sharp edges and corners, which makes the table more pleasing to look at and to touch without changing its shape. It is possible to do this with the random orbital sander but a sanding block is much easier to hold perpendicular than a machine. One final tip: in your vigour to do a job well, do not make the mistake of sanding the bottom of the legs or the buttons. This might disrupt the heights of the leg structure or it could alter the accuracy of the table top fastening. Our table finishing preparation is now complete – it has taken a full day's work to do it properly, but allowing this amount of time has given our wood the respect it deserved. It will also allow the natural beauty of the table to be enhanced further in the next stage – the waxing process.

A quiet hand: the Zen of carpentry

'Fill your bowl to the brim and it will spill. Keep sharpening your knife and it will blunt. Chase after money and security and your heart will never unclench. Care about people's approval and you will be their prisoner. Do your work, then step back. The only path to serenity.'

LAO-TZU

Modern life can be difficult – it moves fast, it feels increasingly complex, it gives us variety but it can make us dizzy with choice, it gives us comforts, but it takes away our great luxury – time. We have learned to be efficient in modern life. We use our time to maximise, we work harder in order to buy new things, to finance fresh experiences. We want to impress people, we want to impress ourselves. We have become very good at planning a good life, but we are not so good at living one. The art of sitting quietly has been replaced by a fear of missing out. It is as though we are continuously running away from the present moment, from the world that is right there in front of us. But we should remember, our struggle to be alone and content with our thoughts is not a modern phenomenon, it is a human condition, a universal conundrum that should be understood and overcome. Carpentry, like all crafts, can help us to reconnect to this simpler world. It can help us to feel more at peace in the present moment and eventually it can show us that perhaps we do not always need to change our life to make it better; sometimes we need to accept it for what it is.

I have certain memories from childhood of how the world looked through my eyes, simple things like the corner of a room or the edge of a table. The world through these eyes is the same but different. It has something to do with the enhanced scale and the closer proximity a child will view objects, but it is also more than this – I can remember the world of possibility, how the tiny details within ordinary household surfaces were transformed into their own vast landscapes. It is difficult to put into words as the image is only part of the story – it is the feeling that is attached to the image that creates the experience. Taking part in the act of carpentry is the closest I have felt to this childhood perspective. It is as though I shrink down my thoughts and the world scales up and with it so too does my sensitivity. It is not a dramatic sensation, it is gentle, not without sound, but free from noise, and although it feels otherworldly, it also feels real.

As adults, our busy lives take over – we can spend days, months or years not engaging closely with the physical world around us and we forget what it feels like. The adult eventually believes their own perspective is the true one, perhaps just because it is the reality they are most in possession of. For me, reconnecting with these surfaces and edges is a way to see the world as we once did. It is also a way to become aware of what Zen sometimes refers to as 'the unborn mind'. The word mindfulness has become a much-used modern term to describe such experiences, but it is a description of a condition that has been expressed for thousands of years.

Just as with meditation, people often consider concepts such as mindfulness or the unborn mind to be mystical or far away. They consider them theories or ideas to be learned and mastered, but it is the opposite. We should think of them as close by, as present everywhere. These concepts are much more about unlearning and remembering to see in the way we once did. These ways of engaging with the world around us are inside all of us, sometimes they just become dormant. The starting point to gain access to a more mindful perspective is to use rituals similar to the ones explained in Part Two. The aim of these rituals is not especially complicated, it is to simply relax you and help you to enjoy your carpentry. The enjoyment is of course important for your mind, but being at peace with your work also helps to improve the quality of your carpentry – the two are very much connected. Whether I am teaching or working alone, I will try to invite a peaceful condition. I even try to discourage things like frowning when concentrating because it is a source of tension. There are many muscles in our face and these muscles not only transfer energy to other parts of our body but they are designed to interact with our thoughts. The focus that comes from enjoyment is more useful than the focus that comes from a fear of making mistakes.

A good carpenter understands how to quickly access these calm states of mind by learning to work in the present moment. They split the processes of table making into a series of manageable tasks and focus on the job at hand. This allows consistency; it becomes irrelevant whether a task is simple or difficult, the pace may slow to accommodate complexity but the application remains the same. The aim is to be the same person throughout, to not force matters, to not allow thoughts to be affected by the outside world, to practise non-duality and be at one with their work.

Many techniques that are used to access a peaceful condition can happen quite naturally when working well. For example, in meditation the traditional way to get in touch with the present moment is to use body movements and breathing to focus your thoughts. Consider for a moment the techniques needed to effectively plane a table top. A rhythm is needed in order to create a smooth and natural flow of movement. The shift of weight through your feet back and forth, the application of force through your muscles and the coordination of your hands and arm movements are all a part of this rhythm and they are all consistent with your breathing pattern. If you compare this to practices such as t'ai chi or yoga then woodwork becomes much the same as an act of meditation.

The improvement of carpentry skills happens gradually. Alongside these skills there should also be an improvement in awareness. Mindfulness and being present in the moment are things that should be practised and cultivated just as carpentry techniques are. To nurture these skills makes them more and more familiar until slowly they become a natural part of how we react to life. When it comes to carpentry and more generally to craft, it is the very act of making which is complicit in developing awareness. The relationship between the task and our thoughts builds an important bridge between the body and the mind – they exist together, one is not more important than the other and the Zen in carpentry shows itself only when we accept that our internal thoughts and the external world are equals.

It is easier to perceive that the tree is the mother of the leaf. We see these grand structures of trunk and branch rise into the world above us to sprout the delicate designs of stem and leaf. We understand that the roots carry water and mineral nutrients from the soil up through the sap to feed these leaves and it seems logical that the tree has grown the leaf. But this is not the full story. Inside every single leaf lies the descendants of the first cell which carried out photosynthesis. The leaf is the power house of any plant, using the sunlight as an energy source to synthesise the building blocks of life. The tree has evolved and exists as a means for leaves to reach higher in the search for light, so it is just as accurate to say the leaf is the mother of the tree.

Humans like order; at times they seem obsessed by classification and hierarchy, but it is being able to see relationships that brings a more complete understanding of life. The carpenter who wishes to improve must become aware of these relationships and connect; it is something that is felt intuitively. They learn to trust themselves, to trust their material, to see wood not as something they need to control, but something they need to be receptive towards. Eventually the master craftsperson becomes more of a conduit, they learn to do less not more, they are able to execute only what is necessary to accomplish a task. It is a kind of doing without doing.

Cast onto the proverbial desert island, my book of choice would be the *Tao Te Ching: The Book of the Way* written by Lao-Tzu (sometimes also known as Laozi). Very little is known about this mysterious figure who lived in China in the sixth century BCE. He left no trace of himself, even his name Lao-Tzu, translated as 'The Old Sage' is uncertain. One of the many legends suggests that he was an archivist at the Zhou court, but left in search of solitude. As he was about to cross the border, one of the guards recognised him and begged for a record of his wisdom. Lao-Tzu wrote the book for him then continued on his way never to be seen again.

LAO-TZU

The Tao Te Ching is a compilation of 81 verse chapters giving advice on how to live harmoniously by following the Tao. The text is often described as enigmatic and amorphous, but I prefer to see it as compelling and intuitive. It is characterised by the practice of '*wu wei*', literally 'non-action'. This is often misunderstood as passivity, but it is better described as the art of acting without interference of the conscious will. The book has a deep wisdom that fits perfectly with the principles of the craftsperson, in the same way an athlete or a dancer becomes lost in their discipline and trusts the intelligence of their bodies; the master carpenter vanishes into the deed and trusts the intelligence of the tree.

I could have chosen any of the eighty-one passages, but here is just one:

Chapter 48

In pursuit of knowledge,
every day something is added.
In the practice of the Tao,
every day something is dropped.
Less and less do you need to force things,
until finally you arrive at non-action.
When nothing is done,
nothing is left undone.
True mastery can be gained
by letting things go their own way.
It can't be gained by interfering.

The table finish: wax, oil and varnish

'Do not plan for ventures before finishing what's at hand.'

EURIPIDES

The one thing above all else that I have learned from carpentry is to 'finish what you start'. I have seen many a beautiful piece of carefully crafted woodwork left to scratch, stain, warp out of shape or even rot, all because of the maker's aversion to the finishing process. With many carpenters, there seems to be a mental barrier towards finishing, perhaps because it is an art in itself, with its own tools and techniques that can feel separate from woodwork. But wood finishing has existed almost as long as woodworking because of the simple fact that any object shaped and cut from wood would simply rot and decay without some form of preservation.

Early Greeks, Egyptians and Romans were all familiar with a variety of preservation techniques. Greeks would use crude vegetable oils to waterproof their boats, Egyptians used shellac and tar as preservative and adhesive while Romans used pitch tar and waxes for preserving their wooden implements. Romans would also char their wood by flame (a practice which has become more associated with Japan) to produce a coating of charcoal which fungi were unable to penetrate. Over the centuries, a variety of resins have been used to preserve wood, many of which are still in use today: Gum arabic from the acacia tree, which is now farmed mostly in Sudan; another resin turpentine which is farmed from various species of pine; shellac which is the resinous secretion of the lac insect *Laccifer lacca* originally from China and India or beeswax which is produced by the female worker honey bee to construct honeycomb cells to store honey and raise their young.

During the 18th century, beeswax and turpentine were readily available and became commonplace in the preservation of favourite objects such as the harpsichord. Beeswax was eventually replaced by French polishing – a shellac and spirit-based mixture which avoided the labour – intensive finish of waxing. The application of French polish developed into a skilled commercial art form. The modern chemically produced preservatives which began to replace organic products began in the 1930s with cellulose and continued with various lacquers, varnishes and oil or water-based urethanes. These types of finish had an advantage over French polishing because of their resistance to water, heat, alcohol, acid and alkaline.

Over the past few decades, modern finishing has been applied by robots, spray guns and surface-coating machines. However, in more recent times it is as though the grain of the wood and the hand of the maker have been rediscovered and there is somewhat of a revival in the more traditional methods. The skills of hand finishing are still basically the same as they were a thousand years ago and they serve the same essential purposes. The most obvious reason to surface coat your table is to beautify the wood but there are many other reasons all of which can be of importance. Finishing will make your table easier to clean and maintain; it will seal the wood which acts as a barrier to moisture and heat changes which can warp your table; it can change the colour and texture of your wood to make it more uniform either with itself or with other furniture; it will preserve your table from wood-eating insects or from decay; and it will prolong the lifespan of your table by increasing its resistance to damage and wear.

Different finishes have different properties some of which will be more beneficial to you than others depending on the type of wood, the use of the table, your expertise in application and your personal aesthetic preferences. There are pros and cons with all finishes, and there are times when you may need to compromise or balance certain aspects or tastes. For example, shellac looks beautiful and it can be easily repaired, but it is not especially easy to apply and it is not water or heat resistant. Oil-based urethane varnishes are very water and heat resistant, they look beautiful on darker woods because they yellow which can blend the colours nicely, but for this reason they seem to spoil the appearance of lighter woods. Water-based urethane varnishes are somewhat less protective but they dry clear which preserves the beauty of a pale wood. However, no varnish is easily repaired, so it is more usual to strip the table completely and start again. Penetrating oils such as Danish oil are easily repaired, easily applied and look very beautiful, but again they can yellow and they are not especially resistant to water or heat.

To help you decide on your final finish it is a good idea to use a test sample on a scrap from your project. Whether through laziness or eagerness to see a finished object, many neglect the simple test sample but a mistake at this point could ruin the look of your table and save you long hours of stripping or re-sanding it down. There are several purposes behind the test sample. It will, of course, help you to understand how your finish will eventually look and feel, but it will also show you any difficulties in the process of application, for example, brush stains, speed of drying or raising of the grain. If you intend to use different layers, such as fillers, stains and topcoats, then the more sophisticated step sample will be useful. This is basically just a scrap that is sectioned off into separate squares so each process can be examined. Either way, you should always write the date and the products used on the back of your various samples as this will avoid any confusion and it will also help you to duplicate the finish should you like it.

In my case I have decided to use beeswax, my logic for which is as follows. In terms of appearance, since my Ash wood was creamy in parts and dark in others, I wanted to accentuate this natural contrast to preserve the story of the wood. Although beeswax has a slightly yellow hue,

I considered it would be just enough to bring out the beauty of the wood. You can buy bleached beeswax, but the process makes it harder and not so supple to apply. As my table was going to be used for just about everything including dining, some people advised me to use a hard varnish such as polyurethane which would stand the rigours of daily life, but I didn't feel as though varnishing really fitted my table. The susceptibility of beeswax to damage is balanced by the ease with which it can be repaired and, in fact, the thought of reapplying beeswax from time to time to maintain the table seemed rather a pleasant idea.

There was also an element of the history and the philosophy of beeswax which appealed. There is no real substitute to beeswax – it is natural, non-toxic and harmless to the skin. I think of it in the same way as I think of olive oil – a little miracle sent from heaven to make our lives on earth a bit better. It can be used in its raw state but it is fairly hard like soap, so for this reason it is normally used in its various composite forms, It is often mixed with pure turpentine, as well as a little ammonia and pumice powder to create a polish. Beeswax has been used by early furniture makers for centuries; it became extensively used in the Tudor period for waxing Oak and with the passage of time, along with the soot and grime of the times, it helped to produce the lovely dark Oak patina which is so sought after by antique dealers. It can also be used as a stopper for small cracks or holes with the help of adding a little colour which I had previously done on a sunken knot on my table.

Rather than just buy the beeswax polish, I decide to continue on my journey of discovery by making it myself. I take a brief break from table making to visit David White, a beekeeper and president of the Northamptonshire Beekeepers' Association. David uses my cousin Robbie's land to make heather honey, a strong, floral and fruity flavoured honey which is high in antioxidants and is therefore prized for its health and healing benefits. Heather honey is made from nectar collected from the tiny purple bell-shaped flower of the common heather plant (*Calluna vulgaris*), so named because of its domination of many areas of heath and moorland. One such heather moorland backs on to Robbie's land and every year, at the end of the summer, David takes up to eighteen hives and places them next to the moors to coincide with the blossoming of this heather. David has kindly offered to supply me with some beeswax which had been made from these Darley Dale bees. This means that the beeswax I will use to preserve my table is made by bees working in the same area as my Ash tree.

I arrive at his house and am greeted at the front door by David followed by a wonderfully intense fragrant aroma of honey. His whole house exudes the life of a beekeeper with extractors, smokers, strainers and various hive parts strewn about his kitchen. We walk past a plethora of jars being honey filled on the way to the garden where bees flit in and out of a selection of different-sized hives. We talk over lunch of all manner of things – the inspirational work ethic of bees, the revival in city rooftop beekeeping and the importance of preserving and passing down information to the next generation. I am reminded that industries such as these are crafts in themselves; beekeeping has many similarities to carpentry, in that it involves a deep historical knowledge that is best learned from person to person and once this knowledge is lost it can take a generation to re-learn the specialist skills involved. Before I go, David talks me through the processes of making my own polish, then he hands me a large chunk of beeswax (for which he kindly wants no payment) and a number of recipes and I leave with the smell of honey in my lungs and the sense of well-being that accompanies generosity.

Back at Darley Dale, armed with my recipes I get down to the task of making my own beeswax polish. There are a few different recipes on my sheets. There is a linseed oil paste polish, a high gloss polish which adds carnauba wax which will polish to a shine, and a leather treatment wax which is a beeswax, tallow and neatsfoot oil mix. I intend to try these recipes out one day, especially the leather treatment, but for my table I decide to make a basic paste polish which is a simple mix of pure turpentine and beeswax. My lump of beeswax weighs in at over a kilogram. I use a knife to chip away smaller flakes until I have just over 250 grams. To melt the beeswax, I use a bain-marie which is a double boiler or two saucepans one on top of the other (you can also use a glass bowl standing in a shallow pan

of water). The bottom pan is filled with water – I use rainwater on David's advice because the chemicals in tap water can discolour the wax. The pan and any utensils should be made from aluminium or stainless steel. Do not use copper or iron because these will also discolour the beeswax. In the top pan I pour 500ml of turpentine, then add the beeswax flakes and gently heat the mixture until the beeswax melts. Beeswax melts from 62 to 66 degrees and the advice from David was not to go too much beyond that for safety reasons. At temperatures over 100 degrees Celsius it will start to vaporise and the risk of it catching fire increases. If anything does catch fire, don't use water to put out the flame, but use a metal lid or a damp cloth as you would when oil catches fire. Within minutes, I have a lovely clear buttercup-coloured liquid, and as you would imagine, the pleasant aroma of beeswax and pine resin fill the kitchen air. Next, I carefully pour the liquid polish through some muslin into a glass jar to take out any impurities giving me the clearest possible finish.

Beeswax retains its temperature for some time, so while the wax is still a little warm and malleable it is easy to get an initial coat over the surface of the whole table. As soon as I begin to apply the polish, the dark-coloured grain contrasts strongly against the creamy white of the light Ash wood. The enhanced beauty of the wood brings with it

a motivation which stands me in good stead for the job that lies ahead. Rubbing beeswax polish into wood takes a lot of elbow grease – I am yet to find an alternative powered method that does the job as well. I do, however, sometimes use my random orbit sander with a high grade of sandpaper to polish up the table once the wax has been sufficiently applied. Upon completion of the first application, I get to work on the next layers. By now the wax polish has dried a creamy primrose colour but it is still surprisingly soft and easy to use. If you are not happy with the consistency of your polish, you can simply add beeswax or turpentine to your mixture to change its viscosity. After a good few hours of *Karate Kid* style waxing on and off, I am satisfied my table is in good shape. As I end the day and turn off the lights, it is impossible not to look back in admiration at the sight of my beautiful new table.

Accepting flaws: the beauty of imperfection

'There is a crack, a crack in everything, that's how the light gets in.'

LEONARD COHEN

There is the sense of an ending now as my table-making experience approaches completion and I cannot help but feel a little sentimental. The making of my table had taken longer than I had expected, but this felt like a good thing – the time had made it feel more like a journey. I suppose I had also become more attached to the table than expected. We had been on the journey together and I had got to know my table, I understood its strengths and its weaknesses but like an old friend, I accepted the whole.

When I stand back and admire my new table, the contrasting colours and unique patterns flowing across its surface, it looks like an object that has quality, but these 'qualities' also contain flaws and imperfections. For example, the majority of the discolouration in my wood is in fact disease; it is probably a particular fungus which affects Ash called *Inonotus hispidus*. This type of discolouration caused by fungi is not uncommon in Ash and is known as spalting. It can occur in many species of trees – spalted Beech is the type I have heard mentioned the most. The fungi produce extracellular pigments inside the wood and the dark winding lines and thin streaks of colour are an interaction zone in which different fungi have erected barriers to protect their resources. Our instincts are to perhaps consider this diseased wood to be of less value, but depending on what the purpose of the wood is, it can be quite highly sought after. A similar type of appreciation is bestowed on burl wood – Walnut trees often bear wart-like protrusions known as burls that produced a swirling pattern. Hundreds of years ago, if you had burl Walnut veneered furniture, this was a real status symbol.

Another easily observable structural 'defect' that can be found in a piece of wood is the knot. A knot can be viewed as a darker, roughly circular shape within the wood grain and it is basically the base of a side branch. Since branches are designed by nature to have the potential to die or drop off then the layers of growth are not so intimately joined. Knots are more likely to crack and they can affect warping. In terms of strength, the weakening effect is much greater when timber is subjected to forces perpendicular to the grain. This is why when wood is used for beams, the number of knots within the wood determines the 'quality' of the wood and therefore its suitability. Once we understand the limitations of a particular flaw, then we can use it in the right way. In the case of a table, the forces involved are unlikely to cause an issue, but knots can be accentuated and exploited for their aesthetic qualities. If my table was made from perfect Ash wood it would be free from any of these imperfections – a creamy, clear table that would be beautiful in its own right, but would I recognise it amongst other tables? Would I grow as fond of it? I can still remember being a young child and staring at our family table, making faces out of the knots and using the waving grain lines as roads for cars. Those shapes are imprinted on my memory and I would recognise that table immediately – it may have been considered a lesser quality wood, but it had more character.

Understanding the purposes of perceived flaws allows us to have a more balanced perspective as nature's weaknesses are often 'designed'. For example, trees that grow in forests, especially dense or closed canopy forests, tend to lose their lower branches as they grow. The lower branches do not receive much sunlight and when this happens, the leaves or needles transpire less, they use less water and they send little or no food towards the main stem of the tree. The tree then cuts off the supply of water and the branch dies. The tree will focus its energy on the growth that is most beneficial to its survival and so this structural 'flaw' of the branch wood acts as a strength in terms of the overall design of the tree, providing a means for the tree to focus its energy in the right places. Nature's weaknesses can also provide important opportunities for others and they exist as part of a more complex ecosystem. For example, the leaves of an Ash tree emerge late because they are not especially hardy. They often wither and die in unseasonal cold snaps, but this late bloom means light will pass through the canopy in spring which allows plants to grow on the forest floor making Ash woods such magical places. Nature has adapted to fill all crevices of the Ash tree's foliar fragility and from the perspective of the plants that grow in these forests, the late bloom is a blessing.

Even from a design or construction perspective, flaws can be viewed positively. For me, the perfection of a mass-produced, machine-manufactured piece loses something along the way, in the same way as a painting that has been over worked or a piece of classical music played by a computer. I look for the hand at work in furniture – the nicks or marks from a hand tool, a fractional miscalculation of a joint, the shallowest of dips where a surface has been over planed. Seeing this hand can be perceived as seeing imperfection, but it opens up a relationship to the maker and makes me care more about the piece. Flaws are not necessarily aspects that should be overcome or hidden, rather they should be understood, accentuated and celebrated. To recognise these flaws, to imagine how a tree has lived, for example, brings us closer to the wood and to the object itself. For me it brings forth a respect or even an empathy and this allows me to see a different kind of beauty in an object.

There is a Japanese term '*wabi-sabi*' which captures these sentiments well – the term is used more and more these days to describe the beauty in imperfection. Just as with '*kogei*', the term does not translate easily. '*Wabi*' was originally used to describe the loneliness of living in nature while '*sabi*' conveyed a sense of something transient and withering. The meaning changed over the centuries and became more positive, so now it is often condensed to 'wisdom in natural simplicity'. The aesthetic of '*wabi-sabi*' can be applied to both natural and human made objects. The characteristics of the aesthetic are asymmetry and roughness, rustic simplicity, modesty, intimacy or natural patina or wear. From a carpentry perspective, the term may be interpreted as the imperfect quality of an object or appreciation of the beauty of age. These aesthetics transcend the object and express sentiments that relate to the human condition. The concept of '*wabi-*

sabi' is actually derived from Buddhist teachings of the three marks of existence – impermanence, suffering and emptiness. To be around natural, changing, unique and imperfect objects helps us to remember that our lives are impermanent This in turn teaches us to connect to the real world, to live through the senses and engage in life as it happens, rather than get caught up in unnecessary thoughts. '*Wabi-sabi*' is, in a way, the material representation of Zen Buddhism.

When I think of imperfection and how we perceive flaws or weaknesses, I see them as concepts that cannot be separated from their positive counterpart. I often think of my strengths as weaknesses and vice versa. The propensity to forget may give us a capacity to heal, while allowing ourselves to be hurt also allows us to love. We cannot control one part of life without it affecting other parts of life and we cannot pick and choose the aspects of ourselves that we want to change without it affecting other aspects of ourselves that we don't want to change. Spanish philosopher and novelist Miguel de Unamuno talks of similar ideas in his book, *Tragic Sense of Life*. He writes that it is the awareness of our mortality which brings us anguish and pain, but also gives us consciousness itself. In some ways it sounds similar to the Buddhist perspective of suffering, but instead of seeing it as something to overcome, Unamuno sees it as an important experience of life. According to him, 'it is only suffering that makes us persons [sic]'. In other words, that experiencing pain allows us to empathise with others and given the choice between either happiness or suffering and love, it is suffering and love which gives life a deeper meaning and significance.

Carpentry has shown me that I cannot pick and choose the properties of wood that I want; that I cannot have beautiful grain without some tensile strength loss, that there is no such thing as perfection, there is only interconnecting manifestations of circumstance. We eventually learn the gentle arts of understanding and acceptance which are the companions of grace. It is these attributes which reveal our own flaws as gifts and allow us to see the connection between imperfection and beauty.

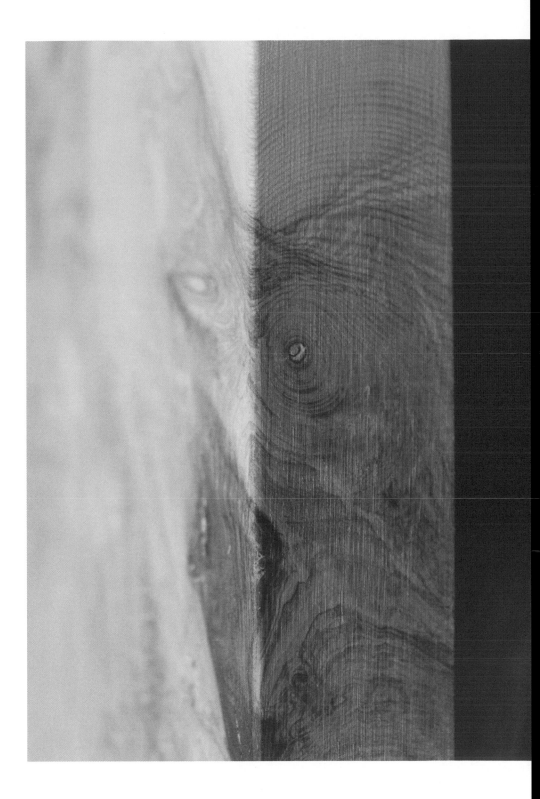

Maintaining your table

'Another flaw in the human character is that everybody wants to build and nobody wants to do maintenance.'

KURT VONNEGUT

An individual's attitude towards maintenance says a lot about their character. Maintenance is similar to preservation; it extends life and expresses respect. In the past, I have fallen prey to a neglectful attitude towards maintenance but it is an essential part of life and the more you participate in it, the easier and more enjoyable it becomes. Whether it is tables, cars, roofs, gardens, personal health or relationships, the sensible among us learn that good maintenance is done in the moment and the longer you leave a problem, the more difficult it will be to solve.

As soon as your table enters your home, it will begin to endure the wear and tear of daily undertakings and with it the inevitable build-up of spillage and scuff across its surface. Depending on the scale of its trials, you may need to consider the reapplication of protective substances. The modern age has seen a perplexing array of creams, waxes, emulsions, oils and sprays enter the market and it has become increasingly difficult to know which one is going to be suitable for your purposes – the answer lies in the type of original finish.

There are various nuances for particular finishes, but generally there are four main options. If you have finished in shellac or French polish then your table should be cleaned with a 'reviver', which usually consists of equal parts of linseed oil, methylated spirits, water, turpentine and white vinegar. After it is cleaned, use a good quality cream or furniture wax. If you have an oil finish to your table, then clean with turpentine and steel wool and re-apply the oil – linseed oil is a good option.

If you have used cellulose-based finishes such as polyurethane or a varnish, then do not use wax or polish, just wash it down with warm water or add a little white vinegar for more stubborn grime. In my case for beeswax, a turpentine and beeswax polish is used to clean and to polish the surface at the same time. A similar logic is used in the repairing of cracks, chips or the opening of grain. Again, the more compatible it is with the original filler then the more successful the repair is going to be. So, oil-based fillers for oil finishes and water-based fillers for water-based finishes. In my case, the beeswax can again be used as filler and as I have previously explained, it is quite simple to add a pigment to match a darker knot of wood.

The great menace of wooden objects, the curse of the cabinet maker, the fear that unites woodworkers around the globe, is the pervasive repercussions of central heating. In the case of your table, avoiding the problems central heating causes is far easier than fixing them – prevention is better than cure. Since wood is a hygroscopic material (it will absorb or release moisture until it reaches an equilibrium with the air that surrounds it), the problem with central heating is that the fast changes in temperature make the wood expand and contract too rapidly causing the wood to crack or split and ruin joints.

There are several countermeasures that are worth considering. You can install a humidifier to preserve moisture content (a cheap version is to put a bowl of water underneath your table from time to time). An easier method is to allow outside air into the room where your table lives so it doesn't get too dry. Never place your table in front of a radiator or obviously an open fire and keep your table well waxed and polished. It is also worth treating the parts of your furniture that will not be seen – treat underneath the table top for example with 50/50 of turpentine and linseed oil. There is no finish that will completely protect your table from shrinkage or expansion, but the idea is that the finish can slow down the process so it is gradual enough to avoid any structural damage. Inspect your table regularly – if you do notice signs of eminent splitting, move the table to allow it to absorb more water and consider a new permanent location if necessary. A good rule to have in your mind is that if you are comfortable, then your furniture should be comfortable also. My table will live in my dining room in which there is only one small radiator – it links to the kitchen which opens onto the back garden. I am hoping the mixture of kitchen boiling and steaming along with the outside air regularly entering the room will act in the same way as a humidifier. The fact that there is not a great deal of direct heat close to the table should also help it to survive. It is advisable to protect your table from standing water and direct sunlight so make good use of heat mats, coasters and curtains.

Protecting the table's structure from things like central heating is non-negotiable in terms of the long-term health of a wooden table, but there are other, practical choices which will influence the way in which my table will be treated in life, choices which are influenced by a philosophy that goes right back to the beginnings of this whole project. I had always wanted my table to participate in the trials and tribulations of family life whatever that entailed; I did not want to worry about the artistic scrawls of an inspired child or the red wine spillages of late-night discussions. I hated the idea of my table entering the realms of the ornament because of the risk of damage – a fear of spoiling a table is a fear of using a table. We all want to preserve the things we like and enjoy for as long as we can and this includes our own lives, but what is the point if this means missing out on all the good things in life? I don't want to be well preserved when my time is up, I want to be thoroughly used up, with nothing else to give and I suppose I have similar aspirations for the life of my table.

A table in the darkness

'Man is the only creature that refuses to be what he is.'

ALBERT CAMUS

I have my table; it stands proudly in front of me ready for a lifetime of work. It is not a perfect table – the discolouration of the spalted wood is evident, the sunken knots in the table have been filled, the bottom rail is slightly bowed due to an early complication of the drying process, but it is definitely a table and it is my table. Encased in the shaped walls of cellulose and lignin is a story – wood is unlike other materials, it bears all, it displays its time on earth in the tight grain of successive hard winters, in the prolonged slow growth of a favourable late summer or in the scars of fungi and fallen branches. I can still see the life of that Ash tree that stood for 160 years on the boundary of two Derbyshire farmlands, before it succumbed to the disease that gradually ate away at its heartwood, resulting in its end.

But there is another story now – over this last eight months we have taken the fallen Ash carcass that lay for nearly a year in the unforgiving weather of that windswept field and set in motion the processes which would give it a new life. The time spent with my cousin in his Darley Dale workshop where we had sawn, carved, drilled, chiselled, planed and sanded this tree, was now also bound within its new form, a form that had the potential to outlast the lifespan of its original living purpose.

My table may not be the perfect table, but it is a good table. The mortise and tenon joints are strong, the legs have an even grain that will keep them from twisting and the table top is tight, even-surfaced and aesthetically unique. But it isn't pretending to be perfect, it isn't pretending to be anything – a table like this knows what it is, it has earned its right through the circumstance and rigorous method of a thousand years of carpentry to stand with pride in any room, ready to be a party to whatever task is asked of it. It is endlessly adaptable, yet always itself and expresses that most elusive of qualities – authenticity with ease.

The humble table has always been there with us, the quiet companion of human kind. It has stood dutifully as scientists and philosophers throughout the ages have scrawled revelations at its surface, but this is not the table's gift to us. Revelations are fleeting moments that change the course of history, but they do not participate in the workings of daily life where we are forced to live for the vast majority of our time. The table's real gift to us is an understanding of the ordinary – it is only an everyday object that can show us the meaning in our everyday experiences.

Such objects communicate from a place that we don't always recognise – they have a subliminal power, you don't see them at work, their magic is invisible. I remember waking one night, in the darkness, from a restless sleep. I went to get a glass of water and I passed our dining-room table on the way to the kitchen. The table stood in its usual silence but it was as if it had a message for me, tidings from a time that had gone. Perhaps it was because I was between sleep and the waking hours, but for the briefest of moments I could see past the world of habit and certainty, I could feel the noiseless presence of truth, and it was reprimanding my soul for not living in the way I had expected to.

A manufactured table, with its clean wood, perfect edges and bolted joints, could not have been the communicator of such a message because the machine-built table represents a different world from that of the hand-built table. Perhaps the manufactured table communicates a message not from the past but from the future. The machines are coming, the automatous economy is already upon us, and artificial intelligence is around the next corner. Just as the machines of the Industrial Revolution began by simulating the hand, and eventually surpassing it, the new machines in their various incarnations will simulate both our physical and our cognitive powers and surpass them.

When we think of what makes humans, it is easy to see the parts that are distinct from other creatures – the capacity to reason, the ability of forethought, our intellectual prowess, the ingenuity to control and alter our environment. But what of the qualities that are distinct from machines – what are the aspects of us that will not be so easily simulated?

Perhaps these are the truest human qualities. I think of all the things that have brought us our philosophy and our art, our imaginations, our fragilities, our deep anxieties, our fear of death, our consciousness of the meaningless condition – these are the things which have allowed us to see the poignancy in our brief lives on Earth and these are the things that have enabled us to feel the whole of time in the seemingly ordinary and innocuous objects that surround us.

Authenticity is more difficult to grasp in humans than in tables, but perhaps it is measured by our capacity to admit what life really is and to accept who we really are. I think this is what the table in the darkness was trying to tell me. A message from the other side, that life is short, and that we should respect and cherish the ordinary moments by being true to ourselves.

The final connection: a table beyond your life

> 'Philosophy is a love-determined movement towards participation in the essential reality of all possibles.'
>
> MAX SCHELER

My table is complete and it is ready to be in the world – the end of creation is always the beginning. All that was left to do was to transport it to its new home. I hired a van for the day as I had been dissuaded from my original plan of loading it onto my roof rack by my cousin Robbie. It did not seem worth the risk of damaging the table, either by strapping it to the roof rack or by exposing it to the elements (the minimum of which would be a 70mph wind from driving down motorways). The journey was three hours long but throughout, there was the sense of travelling with a friend or a family member. I had certainly spent more time in the making of the table than I had with my family lately. The table and I had been through something together – a transformation. The intimate time that is needed to create any object will always build a relationship with the maker and the made.

The table is heavier than I had expected, due in part to the more substantial dimensions (by which I really mean the chunky table top) and it takes two of us to lift it through the house. And there it is, standing in the dining room, in the environment it had been designed and made for – it looks at home. It is at home. The dimensions I had originally designed for the space had changed because of the minor discrepancies in the wood, but to my eyes the table is perfect. There is a generous surface space but still a good amount of room to walk around on all sides. In fact I am glad of the proportion change and I feel the slightly wider width will prove to be useful for a family. The table doesn't overpower, it doesn't withdraw, but it quietly imposes itself which is a good thing. It is a reasonable aspiration for a good table to be the focus of a room.

This had always been the destiny of my table. I had visualised this image before I even started the project and I had set my aim towards it. As part of these imaginings, I had also projected future experiences: I had envisioned my family eating a meal or drawing or doing homework, I had fantasized about late-night drinking or card games with friends, I had even bizarrely invented scenarios in which we were having a family crisis at its surface! I expect in reality I will spend just as much time sitting alone at this table as I do with others. I can be a very solitary man and periods of isolation feel essential to my sense of well-being. I will often imagine happiness alone, but in reality I rarely experience moments of joy sitting with my own thoughts. It may not always feel like it at the time, but the experiences we have with others are precious. Sometimes we absorb the slow gradual interactions that build relationships, at other times we enjoy fleeting connections that remind us who we are. It is often the briefest of moments that we hold on to when we consult our memories.

When I think back to my table-making project and I consider the reasons for starting it in the first place, there is a kind of backdrop to the whole experience. Like the music that defines the tone of a film or the emotion that gives context to a dream, there has always been an accompanying feeling. This feeling has been my companion through careful carpentry, through meetings with like-minded crafters, it is a force that has willed the table's creation and it is still present now in the conclusion of my project, in the real manifestation of my dreams of family life. It is difficult to define, but I suppose if I had to distil it, then the closest meaning I could find in one word would be love. I think at times we misunderstand love, we complicate it and at the same time we limit it. I used to think of love as a word to describe the act of falling in love, but as time goes on in life and our experiences widen, we learn more about its subtleties.

The German philosopher Max Scheler said that, 'Love is a bridge from poorer to richer knowledge.' He is considered part of the phenomenology movement, but he differs from most in his field as rather than focus exclusively on the intellect in examining the structures of consciousness, he wanted to include what he considered to be fundamental to humans – the experience of love or the human heart. Scheler believed that, 'Love opens the spiritual eyes', allowing us to see value, especially the highest possible value, and this determines the way in which we approach the world. Only when reason and logic have love behind them can we achieve philosophical knowledge. At its roots, Scheler is saying that to be human is not just to be a thinking thing, but a being who loves. I often find certain concepts easier to understand if I think of the opposite condition – in the absence of love there is a narrowing of value, our understanding is diminished, we are more closed off to the world. In other words, the greater our capacity for love, the greater our capacity for life.

I had decided to warm the wood of my table with a family meal, to baptise it with experience, to save it from perfection. Our family meals are always pretty lively with two young children and I am immediately forced to put away any worries about spillages. In a sense, the sooner the surface is damaged, the sooner it can get on with its life as a table. At the end of the meal, I make a short toast to all that have helped me bring the table into existence. Shaun and Richard the tree fellers, Pete and the staff from the workshop who made the first cuts, Ken the tree surgeon who told me the story of my Ash tree, David the beekeeper who explained and supplied the beeswax and, of course, my cousin Robbie.

I also make a silent toast to all the philosophers I had read about during the process (silent because my children were already glazing over with the first toast) and I wonder what their perspective might be on the meaning of a simple table. It reminds me of one of those games when people ask, 'If you could have a dinner party with anyone dead or alive, who would you invite?' and Stephen Fry always sits at the head of the table next to David Attenborough and Jesus. There are potentially six places at my table as I will be doing the cooking rather than sitting down. For my dinner party, I would invite a representative from each of the philosophical approaches I have enjoyed: Plato from the rationalists, José Ortega y Gasset from the existentialists, William James from the pragmatists, Hans-Georg Gadamer from the hermeneutics (the study of how humans interpret the world), Hajime Tanabe from phenomenology (the study of consciousness and experience) and Lao-Tzu from Eastern philosophy. This is all the places taken, but I would ask Socrates to help me serve. I think he would help to get Lao-Tzu talking and, besides, it would be nice for him to see Plato again.

It has been my own journey thus far, but it is time for others to get to know my table. I hoped that my family might have a similar affection towards this table as I have to the family table that I grew up with. I wonder if the table will still be here in fifty years' time, or a hundred, or more. It had the potential to be, if treated with respect. It is amusing to consider the future ponderings of a mind at its surface imagining how it would have been to live in the time of Trump, of IKEA furniture and of petrol vans, a time before the robots, when it snowed in Derbyshire and you could still buy beeswax. Just before I had waxed the underside of the table in an effort to maximise its protection against fluctuations in moisture content, I had written a short message which I hoped would remain until its final days.

A TABLE BY JOEL BIRD & ROBERT BALL 2018
THE MAKING OF WHICH IS FEATURED IN A BOOK
'*THE TABLE MAKER*'
MAY IT ENJOY THE GREATEST PRIVILEGE OF ALL
TO BE USEFUL UNTIL THE END OF ITS NATURAL LIFE

It is in some ways comforting to think that my table could outlive me. It is silly really, but we all secretly harbour a longing to be remembered, and the thought of my children reminiscing about times together here, or even someone I didn't know for that matter imagining the hand that made it, is in some ways comforting. It is only really love that survives us, not

A TABLE BY JOEL BIRD & ROBERT BALL
THE MAKING OF WHICH IS FEATURED IN A BOOK
'THE TABLE MAKER'
MAY, IT ENJOY THE GREATEST PRIVILEGE OF ALL
TO BE USEFUL UNTIL THE END OF ITS NATURAL LIFE

just the love we have for people, but the love we have shown in our work. It survives because it is useful, love connects us, it enhances our knowledge, it cultivates our understanding and with this it strengthens our spirit. If love is real, it will be evident and manifest itself in our daily lives. A well-made table is a symbol of this because the qualities that are needed to create such an object are the very same that love provides.

I hope you do make your own table one day. It is a splendid way to learn some of the noble attributes of the maker, but the advice in this book is not just about the making of a table. Whatever it is you do in life, do it well. Look beneath the surface and teach yourself that there is value and beauty in even the most simple and humble of objects. And if you ever get the chance to truly care about something in life, put your heart into it. Because that is what all this is about – respecting the brief amount of time we have here on Earth and expressing that respect with a love for what you do. I like to think this is something my seven imaginary dinner guests might have agreed on.

Our first meal at the table has finished, the table has been cleared, the washing up has been done and the children are in bed. The final and greatest of love's gifts is to connect. As I stand in the fading light of a beautiful spring evening with myself and a cup of tea (on a coaster of course), I can see more than just a table before me. I can see the snowstorm of sawdust from the Alaskan mill streaming into the summer air, the 8-foot antique bandsaw slicing through the slabs. The glue oozing from the mortice holes as the clamps squeezed the tenon shoulders tight against the legs. I can see the flock of redwings flying north as we hand planed our boards in the cold Darley Barn workshop, the burls growing in the place of fallen Ash branches and the Highgate forest trees casting long shadows over Christina Rossetti's gravestone. I can see the ghosts of the early refectory table carpenters who had joined me on a moonlit night, the primitive grasping digits of our arboreal ancestor *Carpolestes simpsoni* and my children's water spillage at our family meal. All parts of the same process, all insignificant, all significant. I sit down at my table quiet, still and solitary just as Kafka had suggested. I am not alone, I am with the world, an unmasked world which now includes my table.

Bibliography

A Dictionary of Philosophy
Antony Flew (Pan 1979)

Flora Britannica
Richard Mabey
(Chatto & Windus, 1996)

Foolproof Wood Finishing
Teri Masaschi
(Fox Chapel Publishing, 2015)

Japonisme
Erin Niimi Longhurst
(Harper Thorsons, 2018)

*Making Authentic
Craftsman Furniture*
Gustav Stickley
(Dover Publications, 1986)

Meditations On Quixote
José Ortega y Gasset
(W. W. Norton & Company, 1963)

Philosophy as Metanoetics
Hajime Tanabe (University
of California Press, 1992)

Pragmatism and Other Writings
William James
(Penguin Classics, 2000)

RHS Botany for Gardeners
Geoff Hodge
(Mitchell Beazley, 2013)

Selected Poems: Rossetti
Christina Rossetti
(Penguin Classics, 2008)

Tao Te Ching
Lao-Tzu (Kyle Cathie, 2000)

The Book of Shed
Joel Bird (Blink Publishing, 2017)

The Dhammapada
Valerie Roebuck
(Penguin Classics, 2010)

The Republic
Plato (Penguin Classics, 2007)

Tragic Sense of Life
Miguel de Unamuno
(Dover Publications, 1976)

Truth and Method
Hans-Georg Gadamer
(Bloomsbury Academic, 2013)

Understanding Wood
R. Bruce Hoadley
(Taunton Press, 2000)

Useful Work v. Useless Toil
William Morris (Penguin, 2008)

Walden
Henry David Thoreau
(Macmillan Collector's Library, 2016)

Wood: Identification and Use
Terry Porter
(GMC Publications, 2006)

Music to
make tables to

Each of us has our own way of working. We make our workspaces feel comfortable, with different tools, temperatures, furniture, lighting or colours, and what we choose to hear is no exception to this. The traditional Japanese workshops famously work in silence, whereas my cousin Robbie likes to listen to his own mix of early millennial house. My own particular preference is to listen to calm acoustic music made by wooden instruments.

There is no substitute for wood; nothing will simulate the resonances which give a characteristic tonal quality to a particular instrument. From the Mahogany used in acoustic guitars, the Maple and Spruce of classical stringed instruments, the Birch wood of drums, the Bamboo of the Japanese shakuhachi or Indian bansuri flutes, the Kiri of the koto or the Toon wood of the sitar. Often there is a mixture of woods in one instrument, take the piano which may consist of a Spruce soundboard, Maple bridges and pin block, Fir keys, with any number of different wood varieties making the framework and exterior case. Even the brass saxophone owes its sound to the resonating reed made from Arundo donax (Giant Cane), as do all woodwind instruments. Consider for a moment what the history of music would be like without these instruments.

Musical instrument making is a highly skilled craft and when I listen to this type of music I understand I am listening to the sounds of pieces made by specialised carpenters. I find it all adds to the experience and sometimes I think it subconsciously gets me in tune with wood. So with this in mind, here is a short list of some of my favourite music to make tables to.

Ali Farka Touré & Toumani Diambaté: *In the Heart of the Moon*

Bill Evans Trio: *Sunday at the Village Vanguard*

J. S. Bach (Yo-Yo Ma): *Cello suites No. 1, 5 & 6*

Various (Shin-ichi Fukuda): *Japanese Guitar Vol. 2*

Bob Dylan: *Pat Garrett & Billy the Kid*

Mozart (Walter Klien): *Mozart Piano Sonatas Vol. 1 & 2*

Shivkumar Sharma, Brijbushan Kabra & Hariprasad Chaurasia: *Call of the Valley*

Miles Davis: *Kind of Blue*

Various: *Sakura – A Musical Celebration of the Cherry Blossoms*

Franz Schubert (Emerson String Quartet): *String Quintet in C*

Smoke and Mirrors Percussion Ensemble: *Smoke and Mirrors*

Acknowledgements

Thank you to Shaun and Richard from Natural Earth Woodcraft, Pete and staff from Ashton & Coleman, Ken from Emery Landscapes, David from Northamptonshire Beekeepers' Association, and especially my cousin, Robert Ball. It has been a privilege to work with such talented people and without their knowledge and generosity my table-making project would not have been possible.

I would also like to thank all those who preserve the relevance of traditional crafts and endeavour to pass on the skills and knowledge of their work to the next generation.

Say hello or tell me of your own table-making experience via @MrJoelBird and visit www.joelbird.com